VICTORIAN NOVEL ILLUSTRATION

GARLAND REFERENCE LIBRARY
OF THE HUMANITIES
(VOL. 164)

VICTORIAN NOVEL ILLUSTRATION
A Selected Checklist 1900–1976

John Charles Olmsted
Jeffrey Egan Welch

GARLAND PUBLISHING, INC. • NEW YORK & LONDON
1979

Library of Congress Cataloging in Publication Data

Olmsted, John, 1942–
  Victorian novel illustration.

  (Garland reference library of the humanities ; 164)
  Includes indexes.
    1. English fiction—19th century—Illustrations—
Bibliography. I. Welch, Jeffrey, joint author. II. Title.
Z5956.I44045   [NC978]   016.74164′0942   78-68248
ISBN 0-8240-9773-4

Printed on acid-free, 250-year-life paper
Manufactured in the United States of America

For Margery

CONTENTS

PREFACE

This bibliography lists and annotates books and articles treating British novel illustration of the Victorian period published from 1900 to 1976. Items are arranged chronologically and are alphabetized by the author's name within each year. Anonymous articles are listed alphabetically by title at the beginning of the entries for each year. Annotations employ the author's own words in order to give both a summary of the content and a means of gauging the significance of each item. More important items are extensively annotated. All books and articles listed have been examined; in the few cases where an item could not be located, the entry is marked "not seen." Annotations of doctoral theses are derived from the author's description published in *Dissertation Abstracts*. The original publisher of each book is given; in cases of simultaneous publication in Great Britain and the United States, the American publisher is indicated.

We have attempted to list all articles of any significance treating aspects of British novel illustration in the period between 1825 and 1900. Articles dealing exclusively or primarily with other aspects of book illustration, such as the illustration of travel books or of books of poetry, have been excluded. Writings treating the illustration of children's books have also been largely excluded, although we have listed a few important articles and books on the subject which treat theoretical issues concerning the relationship between artist and illustrator in a particularly revealing manner.

The focus of the bibliography naturally reflects the focus of scholarly work on novel illustration. The relationship between Dickens and his illustrators is the subject of the bulk of these writings, although good work on Thackeray as illustrator has begun to appear.

We have included listings of important bibliographies of the works of Dickens, Trollope and Thackeray which include information about the illustrations. We do not list library and exhibition catalogues unless they contain information not easily available elsewhere.

The appendices list important illustrated novels of the period and provide short biographical sketches of the more prolific illustrators. The index is divided into two parts: the first lists the authors of critical articles and books; the second lists novelists, illustrators, illustrated novels and issues and concepts dealt with in the criticism.

We wish to thank the Graduate Library at the University of Michigan, the Princeton University Library, the Yale University Library and the Michigan State Library for access to their collections. Cathryn Camper worked for several months researching and verifying items in the bibliography; we are grateful for her help. Linda L. Clarke prepared the final typescript.

Finally, we wish to express our appreciation to Dean Robert Longsworth of Oberlin College and Professor Robert H. Super of the University of Michigan for their encouragement and support.

J.C.O.
J.W.

INTRODUCTION

Modern readers most often encounter Victorian fiction in paper-back versions or, at best, in those dusty turn-of-the-century sets acquired from secondhand book sellers. In neither case are they experiencing the novel as the original author intended. Questions of the corruption of the text itself aside, the main problem with most published versions of the fiction of nineteenth-century Britain is that they do not contain the many plates and inserted woodcuts which were a part of the first published parts or installments of the novels of Dickens, Thackeray, Ainsworth, Lever, Trollope and Hardy. Even in cases where illustrations were included in modern reprints, they were often drawn by artists of a later period. It is only in the past ten to fifteen years that scholars and general readers alike have begun to investigate and enjoy that unique "interdisciplinary" artifact, the Victorian illustrated novel.

Readers at the beginning of this century, however, were for the most part content that the editions of Dickens that they used were not defaced by the "caricatures" of Hablot K. Browne or George Cruikshank. A typical Dickensian, W.A. Fraser, wrote in 1906 [15]

> Not even the most indulgent critic can seriously assert that Dickens ever received really adequate artistic assistance in any of his novels, with the exceptions of *Our Mutual Friend* and *Edwin Drood*. Hablot Browne was not a genius or even a great artist, and George Cruikshank was a mere caricaturist of the bad old school of Gillray and Rowlandson. John Leech and Doyle contributed to the Christmas Books only.

Contempt for adherents to that "bad old school" of early nineteenth-century illustration continued until at least the late 1930s. For one observer, Thackeray is "devoid of technique" [2] as an illustrator; Richard Doyle is praised for his "refinement," but readers are warned that it would be a mistake to separate the artist from his "proper sphere of decoration" [5]. The illustrations of H.K. Browne were defended by his son in a memoir [29], but in terms that were scarcely flattering: "For a young man, imperfectly trained in the art of drawing, it was easier to succeed in the grotesque than in the beautiful." Several assumptions run through all of these disparaging references to the illustrators of Dickens. All of the writers treat the illustrations as excrescences, visual aids designed for an unimaginative audience. All assume as well that Dickens was an unwilling collaborator, unhappy with the prevailing fashion for illustrated serial fiction. The early unhappy collaboration with Robert Seymour and R.W. Buss and the uneasy relationship Dickens had with Cruikshank were pointed to as evidence of Dickens' reluctance to share his pages with a comic illustrator.

Only G.K. Chesterton of Dickens' early twentieth-century critics recognized that the collaboration of novelist and illustrator could result in a new kind of hybrid art form [14]. His description of Cruikshank's famous drawing of Fagin awaiting his execution recognizes the peculiar identity of imagination in Cruikshank and Dickens:

> There was about Cruikshank's art a kind of cramped energy which is almost the definition of the criminal mind. His drawings have a dark strength: yet he does not only draw morbidly, he draws meanly. In the doubled-up figure and frightful eyes of Fagin in the condemned cell there is not only a baseness of subject; there is a kind of baseness in the very technique of it. It is not drawn with the free lines of a free man; it has the half-witted secrecies of a hunted thief. It does not look merely like a picture of Fagin; it looks like a picture by Fagin.

The bulk of the references to illustrated fiction in the 1920s and 1930s were biographical and anecdotal in nature. Several critics championed Robert Seymour and the "unfortunate" R.W. Buss. The popularity of *The Pickwick Papers* drew many critics to an examination of the unique circumstances surrounding its early history. But the conflict between Seymour and Dickens, and

Dickens' molding of H.K. Browne into a docile collaborator, were treated as circumstances of only peripheral importance.

It was not until 1937 with the announcement of the appearance of the Nonesuch Dickens that interest in the illustrations as an integral part of the experience of reading Dickens became apparent. Arthur Waugh, in a prospectus [101] for the new edition, argued the importance of the work of "Phiz" and company: "The original Dickens illustrations are an integral part of the Dickens stories, almost as closely allied with the author's appeal as the text itself." In the same year Sacheverell Sitwell focused on the collaboration of Dickens with Cruikshank, crediting the artist with making the whole of Dickens "visible" [106].

In a subsequent series of articles in *The Dickensian* [116, 123, 127], Thomas W. Hill argued for the importance of the illustrations largely on the grounds that Dickens had contrived to include illustrations and therefore they must be taken into account. Although sympathetic to the work of Browne, Hill valued him as a passive extension of Dickens' imagination. The idea that "Phiz" might be adding something to the novels from his own imaginative stores does not seem to have occurred to Hill. Indeed, in most of the critical writings on novel illustration until the late 1960s, the standard that has been applied has been one of a kind of mimetic appropriateness to the text. The idea of a dynamic relationship between two creative personalities is a recent one.

A series of critical monographs published in 1948 suggested a revival of interest in novel illustration. Daria Hambourg's fine little book on Richard Doyle [152], Ruari McLean's study of George Cruikshank as book illustrator [153] and Derek Pepys Whiteley's monograph on George du Maurier [157] all treated the collaboration of artist and novelist as an attempt to fuse art forms in a new and remarkable way.

The publication in 1957 of John Butt and Kathleen Tillotson's study [183] of Dickens' habits of composition marked a new and promising direction in the study of illustrated novels with its emphasis on the integral part that the illustrations played in Dickens' planning for his novels. In 1965 the importance of Thackeray's illustrations to his text was once again argued [205] and in the following year Donald Hannah made modest claims for

Thackeray's drawings as appropriate "accompaniment to the action" of his fiction [207].

In the same year the first of Michael Steig's remarkable investigations of the relationship between Dickens and his illustrators appeared [209]. Combining insights gained from Freudian psychological theory with a sound knowledge of the traditions of graphic satire in late eighteenth- and early nineteenth-century England, Steig argued that the illustrations were more than just an amusing visual accompaniment to a novel's text. By treating the "Dickens-Browne" novel as a unified creation Steig was able, in an article published in 1969 [228], to suggest the ways in which author and visual artist grew as creative artists from the same tradition of visual satire:

> Browne's illustrations to Dickens' novels . . . like the novels' texts themselves, display a development from an essentially caricatural style to a more complex and realistic one, as well as a gradual development of techniques for expressing a sweeping vision of the dehumanization of man's world.

In 1970 Steig argued that Browne often added supportive elements of allegory and symbol in his illustrations to the novels without prompting from Dickens. This made the illustrations take on a special significance as "a kind of running commentary on the text," embodying "a consistent visual symbolism" [243].

Complementary to Steig's researches was the important work of Robert L. Patten. His reading of Browne's frontispiece to *The Pickwick Papers* [213], a review [214] of Kathleen Tillotson's Clarendon edition of *Oliver Twist* and an important article focusing on a Browne plate in *Pickwick* [227] all reflected his conviction that the heritage of graphic representation originating in Hogarth had shaped the imaginations of both Dickens and Browne. John Dixon Hunt, in an essay published in 1971 [254], came close to reversing the old belief in the subservience of Dickens' illustrators. Instead, Hunt argues, "Dickens drew upon and was conditioned by the same graphic traditions that gave him his illustrators." Further,

It would appear that such early works as the *Sketches* and *Pickwick Papers* were directly nourished by the world of graphic journalism and that the large readership Dickens soon commanded is perhaps a measure of his success in extending into literary form the topics, treatment and attitudes of popular engravings.

Only two books have dealt directly with the issues raised by the study of illustrated novels. J.R. Harvey's 1970 survey [235] of serial illustrated fiction in the 1830s, 1840s and 1850s argued persuasively for the view that "text and picture *can* truly work together." While the illustrations of Cruikshank and Browne could vividly suggest character and mood, they could do much more; "they could develop a novel's themes subtly, delicately, and powerfully, and in essentially visual terms." The second book-length study, a collection of essays on George Cruikshank edited by Robert L. Patten, contained some of the best criticism published to this date on the relationship between what some partisans might argue only half in jest to be the relationship between a great illustrator and his novelists. Essays by Anthony Burton [274], Louis James [282], Ronald Paulson [291], Michael Steig [294], Harry Stone [297] and Richard A. Vogler [299] examined in detail the nature and significance of Cruikshank's work as an illustrator.

Yet despite able scholarly work, Victorian illustrated novels have scarcely begun to be examined carefully. Recent arguments for the significance of John Everett Millais' illustrations [313] and for the importance of the largely forgotten illustrators of Thomas Hardy [290] suggest entirely new areas of investigation. Book-length studies of H.K. Browne and George Cruikshank are promised, but so far investigations have remained for the most part tentative and narrow. At a time when so much published criticism still moves over well-travelled ground, it is heartening to see in the study of Victorian novel illustration a wholly new and exciting area for inquiry.

J. C. O.

THE BIBLIOGRAPHY

1   Dalziel, George and Edward. *The Brothers Dalziel.*
      A Record of Fifty Years' Work in Conjunction
      with Many of the Most Distinguished Artists of
      the Period 1840-1890. London: Methuen.

      Account of the firm that produced engravings
for many Victorian illustrators.

2   Hobbs, William Herbert. "Art as the Handmaid of
      Literature." *The Forum* 31: 370-82.

      "The edition of Dickens illustrated by that
famous coterie of artists which included Cruikshank,
Seymour, 'Phiz,' Cattermole, Leech, Darley, Gilbert,
Doyle, Tenniel, Landseer, Palmer, Stanfield, and
several others, presents perhaps as remarkable an
array of pictures as can be found in the works of
any novelist. It is, I believe, a somewhat popular
impression that these drawings are also in a remarkable degree successful...While it cannot be denied
that many of them are truly admirable, there are
others which are gross exaggerations or even caricatures, and I cannot believe that they correctly set
forth the writer's conceptions."

      "Thackeray was...so absolutely devoid of tech-
nique that his illustrations, even when worked over
by Walker, were nearly always failures."

3   Wilson, R. R. "Tenniel and His Work." *The Critic*
         38: 141-48.

                            1902

4   Bamburgh, William Cushing. "Some Letters of
         'Phiz.'" *The Book Buyer* 23 (January): 542-45.

     Two letters from H. K. Browne.

     "Browne's art, when united with Dickens's word-
     pictures, produced a combination full of rare
     genius--more remarkable than the union of Cruikshank
     with Dickens in *Oliver Twist*."

5   Lusk, Lewis. "The Best of Richard Doyle." *The Art
         Journal*: 248-52.

     "Doyle has rarely been taken seriously as an
     artist."

     As an illustrator Doyle "can generally be
     sufficiently in sympathy with his author, if not
     required to be strenuous, grim, or realistic."

     "One must not separate Doyle too far from his
     style, which belongs to graceful fancy, not to
     awkward fact; you must not take him from his proper
     sphere of decoration, and set him to work at realism
     with its tones and values. Give him a gracious idea
     to put into decorative fancy, and he did it with a
     refinement peculiar in its simplicity."

6   Matz, B. W. "Dickens and his Illustrators." *The
         Critic* 40: 43-46.

     In his collaboration with his illustrators
     Dickens "knew what he wanted, and insisted upon hav-
     ing it."

                             4

1903

7   Douglas, Captain R. J. H. *The Works of George
     Cruikshank. Classified and Arranged With
     References to Reid's Catalogue and Their
     Approximate Values.* London: J. Davy & Sons.

     Includes a listing of novels illustrated by
Cruikshank.

8   Kitton, F. G. *Dickens and His Illustrators.* A
     paper read at the inaugural meeting of the
     Dickens Fellowship, held in London, November
     5th, 1902. London: The Dickens Fellowship.

9   Sketchley, R. E. D. *English Book-Illustration of
     Today: Appreciations of the Work of Living
     English Illustrators With Lists of Their Books.*
     Introduction by Alfred W. Pollard. London:
     Kegan Paul, Trench, Trübner.

10   Smith, W. Brooke. "Four Thackeray Sketches."
     Harper's Magazine 107: 427-31.

     Sketches Thackeray made as a boy suggest some
of the concerns of his later novel illustrations.

1904

11   Melville, Lewis. "Thackeray and His Illustrators."
     *Books and Bookplates: The Book-Lover's
     Magazine* 5 (1904-05): 278-98.

12   Melville, Lewis. "Thackeray as Artist." *The
     Connoisseur* 8: 29-31, 152-55.

"Thackeray himself always declared that, although he was not a first-rate artist, he was not
half so bad as the woodcutters made him appear.
And an inspection of his drawings supports this view.
Certainly, though he lacked academic correctness
and technical mastery, the undeniable originality
and humour of his sketches will secure for them a
very long lease of life."

1905

13   Saint-Gaudens, Homer.   "John Leech." *The Critic*
        47: 358-67.

        Brief account of Leech's career.

1906

14   Chesterton, G. K. *Charles Dickens*.   London:
        Methuen.

        Brief commentary on illustrations.

        It is "a strange and appropriate accident" that
Cruikshank and not Browne should have illustrated
Oliver Twist.

        "There was about Cruikshank's art a kind of
cramped energy which is almost the definition of
the criminal mind. His drawings have a dark
strength: yet he does not only draw morbidly, he
draws meanly. In the doubled-up figure and fright-
ful eyes of Fagin in the condemned cell there is not
only a baseness of subject; there is a kind of baseness in the very technique of it. It is not drawn
with the free lines of a free man; it has the half-
witted secrecies of a hunted thief. It does not
look merely like a picture of Fagin; it looks like
a picture by Fagin."

15   Fraser, W. A. "The Illustrators of Dickens." *The
          Dickensian* 2: 117-22 (George Cruikshank);
          176-83 (Hablot K. Browne); 237-39 (George
          Cattermole); 263-66 (Marcus Stone); 330-33
          (John Leech and the Christmas Books). See
          reply, 17.

      "It is a commonly expressed opinion nowadays
that the works of Dickens have never been adequate-
ly and suitably illustrated, that most of the
artists employed originally caricatured rather than
portrayed the chief personages in the books. In
this series of articles it is proposed to deal with
the work of Dickens's illustrators from a critical
point of view as they appear in the light of modern
taste."

      "Not even the most indulgent critic can seri-
ously assert that Dickens ever received really
adequate artistic assistance in any of his novels,
with the exceptions of *Our Mutual Friend* and *Edwin
Drood*. Hablot Browne was not a genius or even a
great artist, and George Cruikshank was a mere
caricaturist of the bad old school of Gillray and
Rowlandson. John Leech and Doyle contributed to
the Christmas Books only."

      Cruikshank would "have been quite forgotten by
this time were it not for his long association with
the masterpieces of Dickens."

16   Philip, Alex J. "Blunders of Dickens and his
          illustrators." *The Dickensian* 2: 294-96.

      "Probably Dickens suffered more at the hands
of his illustrators than any other of our great
novelists."

17   White, Kay. "Cruikshank, 'Phiz,' and Modern Taste."
          The Dickensian 2: 239-40. Response to
          Fraser's criticisms of the original Dickens
          illustrators, 15.

      Dickens was well served by his illustrators.

1907

18   Layard, George Somes. *Suppressed Plates Wood En-*
        gravings, &c. Together with Other Curiosities
        Germane Thereto Being an Account of Certain
        Matters Peculiarly Alluring to the Collector.
        London: Adam and Charles Black.

        Suppressed and cancelled illustrations by
        Thackeray, Cruikshank, R. W. Buss and others.

1908

19   Boswell, Clarence. "Charles Dickens as an Artist."
        The Dickensian 4:   69-72.

        Dickens' own drawings of several of his
        characters.

20   Chesson, W. H. *George Cruikshank.*   London:
        Duckworth.

        Account of Cruikshank's career with commentary
        on his illustrations for Ainsworth, Dickens and
        others.

21   Fraser, W. A. "Sir Luke Fildes's Illustrations to
        Edwin Drood: An Appreciation." *The Dickensian*
        4:   41-43.

        "The illustrations of *Edwin Drood* are as nearly
        perfect as black-and-white work ever can be."

1909

22   Dobson, Austin. "The Oxford Thackeray." *National
         Review* 52: 794-802. Reprinted in *Old
         Kensington Palace, and Other Papers*. London:
         Chatto & Windus, 1910, 271-89. A review-essay
         treating George Saintsbury's edition, *The
         Oxford Thackeray*.

         Thackeray's illustrations to the novels are
      "part of the author's intellectual output, and,
      where they illustrate his writings, represent, more
      nearly than it would be possible for any second
      person to represent, what he wished to convey to
      his readers."

1910

23   Hammerton, Sir John A. *The Dickens Picture Book:
         A Record of Dickens Illustrators*. Vol. 17 of
         Works of Charles Dickens. Ed. Sir John A.
         Hammerton. 18 vols. London: Educational Book
         Co.

24   Ley, J. W. T. "Robert William Buss: A Tribute to
         an Unlucky Artist." *The Dickensian* 6: 33-37,
         71-75.

         Account of Buss's attempt to illustrate
      Pickwick Papers.

1911

25   "Thackeray as Artist." *Academy* 80: 623-24.

         In his drawings, "Thackeray never falls into
      that savage grossness of caricature which to the
      modern eye spoils so much of the work of his

contemporaries." Thackeray's illustrations for his
essays and burlesques are superior to those he drew
for the novels. "Thackeray as artist was incapable
of the same serious flights as Thackeray the author."

26   Ellis, S. M. *William ·Harrison Ainsworth and His
      Friends*. 2 vols. London: John Lane.

      Contains information about Ainsworth's collab-
oration with his illustrators, among them
Cruikshank, Frederick Gilbert, R. W. Buss, H. K.
Browne and others.

27   Melville, Lewis. *Some Aspects of Thackeray*.
      Boston: Little, Brown.

      "There has rarely been an artist who made his
drawings so helpful to the text. Indeed, the
characters are depicted as truly by the pencil as
by the pen, and they tell the story together."

1912

28   Wilson, Stanley Kidder. "News for Bibliophiles."
      Nation 95: 479-80.

      A list of works illustrated by John Leech.

1913

29   Browne, Edgar. *Phiz and Dickens*. London: James
      Nisbet.

      Recollections of H. K. Browne by his son.

      Contains an account of his career as
illustrator.

"For a young man, imperfectly trained in the
art of drawing, it was easier to succeed in the
grotesque than in the beautiful, for the one needs
only approximate correctness, but the other depends
entirely on good draughtsmanship for the realisation
of an ideal. We therefore find him in the early
Dickens books pushed on by circumstances into the
position of caricaturist, and it is not surprising
that the glimpses of beauty are so infrequent and
modest, but rather that there were any at all. The
public did not ask for them, but there seems reason
to suppose that they had an effect in insinuating a
taste which for some time to come was latent and not
acknowledged."

30   Jackson, Holbrook. *The Eighteen Nineties. A Review
        of Art and Ideas at the Close of the Nineteenth
        Century.* London: Jonathan Cape.

     Brief treatment of the theory and practice of
book illustration in the 1890s.

31   Wood, T. Martin. *George Du Maurier, The Satirist
        of the Victorians. A Review of His Art and
        Personality.* New York: McBride, Nast.

     Account of his career as illustrator of his own
fiction and of the works of others.

1914

32   Cohn, Albert M. *A Bibliographical Catalogue of the
        Printed Works Illustrated by George Cruikshank.*
        London: Longmans, Green.

11

1915

33   Cohn, Albert Mayer. *A Few Notes Upon Some Rare
     Cruikshankiana.* London: Karslake & Company.

34   Ley, J. W. T.   "Boz and Phiz: Centenary of Hablot
     Knight Browne's Birth." *The Dickensian* 11:
     145-53.

     "Personally, I would rather have one of
     Barnard's illustrations than ten of Browne's--that
     is, of course, putting aside all considerations of
     sentiment; and my own view is, that if *Pickwick* were
     being issued to-day, Phiz's illustrations would not
     be tolerated.   In later books he improved, but, with
     at most, few exceptions, he never did anything near-
     ly so good as Luke Fildes's illustrations to *Edwin
     Drood.*"

35   Matz, B. W.   "'Phiz'.   The Centenary of Hablot
     Knight Browne." *The Bookman* 48 (June):   69-74.
     Not seen.

1916

36   Ellis, S. M.   "Thackeray's Illustrations: Their
     Personal and Topographical Interest." *The
     Athenaeum* (September):   403-06.   Reprinted in
     Mainly Victorian. London: Hutchinson, 52-66.

     "Thackeray was certainly a greater author than
     artist; but he remains the most interesting example
     of a novelist who was able to illustrate his own
     literary creations with drawings very humorous,
     quaint, and pathetic: drama and horror and passion
     were beyond the reach of his pencil in the same
     successful degree, and when he did essay them, on
     rare occasions, he treated them with a bizarre
     touch."

37   Maurice, Arthur Bartlett. "Cruikshank in America."
            The Bookman 44: 288-98.

        The Meirs Collection of Cruikshankiana at
    Princeton described. Cruikshank's work as novel
    illustrator evaluated.

                            1917

38   Ley, J. W. T. "John Leech: Dickens's Friendship
            With the Great *Punch* Artist." *The Dickensian*
            13: 202-07.

        Leech would have been a better illustrator for
    Pickwick Papers than Browne.

                            1918

39   C., F. "Tenniel's Book-Illustrations." *Notes and
            Queries* (September): 237-38.

        List of books illustrated by Sir John Tenniel.

40   Rosenbach, A. S. W. *A Catalogue of the Works
            Illustrated by George Cruikshank and Isaac and
            Robert Cruikshank in the Library of Harry
            Elkins Widener.* Philadelphia: Privately
            printed.

                            1919

Van Duzer, Henry Sayre. *A Thackeray Library: First Edi-
            tions and First Publications Portraits Water
            Colors Etchings Drawings and Manuscripts. A
            Few Additional Items are Included, Forming A
            Complete Thackeray Bibliography.* New York:

                            13

Privately Printed. Reprinted in 1965 by the
Kennikat Press, Port Washington, New York with
a new introduction by Lionel Stevenson.

"This volume describes a complete set of the
First Editions and First Publications of Thackeray's
writings in book form, and in the magazines, news-
papers and periodicals of England and the United
States. It is arranged as a Bibliography of first
publications, and all items not contained in the
Library are indicated by a star."

In his introduction, Lionel Stevenson calls
Van Duzer's claim to have produced a complete
bibliography "specious" but adds that despite the
omissions and inconsistencies of the catalogue "it
can defend itself complacently with the simple
retort that it is indispensable."

42   Wilkins, William Glyde. "Variations in the
        Cruikshank Plates to Oliver Twist." *The
        Dickensian* 15: 71-74.

1920

43   Matchett, Willoughby. "How Dickens's Two Drood
        Secrets were Hidden in the Cover-Design." *The
        Dickensian* 16: 31-36.

Clues to the outcome of *Edwin Drood* in Charles
Collins' cover design for the original wrappers.

44   Wilkins, William Glyde.   "Cruikshank Versus Dickens."
        The Dickensian 16: 80-81.

Cruikshank's claim that he suggested many of
the subjects for Dickens' *Sketches by Boz* discussed.

1921

45   "Dickens's Instructions to Phiz." *The Dickensian*
           17: 94-95.

           Dickens' directions to Browne for the illustra-
      tions to *Martin Chuzzlewit*.

46   Sullivan, Edmund J. *The Art of Illustration*.
           London: Chapman and Hall.

           Some mention of novel illustration.

1923

47   Spencer, Walter T. *Forty Years in My Bookshop*.
           London: Constable.

           Anecdotal commentary on many Victorian novel
      illustrators, among them Cruikshank, Browne and Luke
      Fildes.

1924

48   Cohn, Albert M. *George Cruikshank: A Catalogue
           Raisonné of the Work Executed During the Years
           1806-1877; With Collations, Notes, Approximate
           Values, Facsimiles, and Illustrations*.
           London: *Bookman's Journal*. See notes and
           corrections, 143.

49   Parker, Robert Allerton. "The Great George." *The
           Arts* 6: 210-24.

           The work of Cruikshank assessed.

"What surprises us today is not so much the
triumphant popularity of the great George, as the
high quality of his engraving and draughtsmanship."

50   Surtees, R. S., and E. D. Cuming. *Robert Smith
          Surtees (Creator of 'Jorrocks')*. London:
          Blackwood and Sons.

      A biography with information about Surtees'
collaboration with John Leech and other illustrators.

                        1925

51   Irwin, Mary Leslie. "Anthony Trollope: A Biblio-
          graphy." *Bulletin of Bibliography* 12 (May,
          1924- December, 1925): 71-73, 92-96, 114-16,
          150-55. Revised and reprinted as *Anthony
          Trollope: A Bibliography*. New York: H. W.
          Wilson Co., 1926. Reprinted New York: Burt
          Franklin, 1968.

      A bibliography of Trollope's writings and an
annotated check-list of biographies and criticism
of the novelist.

52   Ley, J. W. T. "Robert Seymour and Mr. Pickwick."
          The Dickensian 21: 122-27.

      The claim of Seymour's widow that her husband
had invented the character Pickwick in *Pickwick
Papers* assessed.

53   Locke, Harold. *A Bibliographical Catalogue of the
          Periodical Novels and Ballads of William
          Harrison Ainsworth*. London: Elkin Mathews.

                        16

54   Thackeray, William Makepeace. *A Book of Drawings.*
          A Series of Metamorphoses made in Philadelphia,
          1853, for the Children of William B. Reed.
          With a Note by Agnes Repplier. Philadelphia,
          Pa.: The Pennell Club.

                              1926

55   Walmsley, Elizabeth. "'New Lamps for Old':
          Charles Dickens on Art." *The Cornhill Magazine*
          ns 60: 203-12.

          Dickens' art criticism assessed.

          "He knew something about pictures, and despite
       his being very wrong in good company in 1850, the
       principles of criticism that he held--that art
       should be beautiful before all things else, and that
       art should have a noble purpose--have been endorsed
       by a great weight of authority since."

          "The story of Dickens's relations with his
       illustrators...throws little light on his views upon
       art. He was seldom exercised about the execution
       of his illustrations, only keenly concerned as to
       their correspondence with the text. Of all his
       illustrators, Mr. Luke Fildes interpreted his fancy
       most faithfully and with the greatest sympathy."

                              1927

56   Gadd, W. Laurence. "Sir Luke Fildes and *Edwin
          Drood.*" *The Dickensian* 23: 157-60.

          Notes on Fildes' illustrations to the Dickens
       novel.

57   Gaunt, William. "Millais the Illustrator." *Drawing
          & Design*: 95-100. Not seen.

58   Latimer, Louise P. "Illustrators: A Finding List."
        Bulletin of Bibliography 13: 27-29, 46-48,
        74-75, 94-95. Printed as *Bulletin of Biblio-*
        graphy Pamphlet No. 27. Revised as *Illustra-*
        tors. Useful Reference Series, No. 39, 1929.

59   Locke, Harold. "First Editions among the Cheap
        Issues of Mid-Victorian Days." *The Bookman's*
        Journal 15:   185-88.

        Cheap illustrated parts editions of Victorian
        novels by publishers like John Dicks and Vickers
        discussed.

60   Roe, F. Gordon. "Portrait Painter to 'Pickwick;' or,
        Robert Seymour's Career." *The Connoisseur* 77:
        152-57.

        Brief account of Seymour's career.

61   Roe, F. Gordon. "Seymour, the 'Inventor' of
        '*Pickwick.*'" *The Connoisseur* 77:   67-71.

        Examines the claims of Seymour's wife that the
        conception and design of the work were wholly the
        invention of her husband.

                             1928

62   Eckel, John C. *Prime Pickwicks in Parts. Census*
        with Complete Collation Comparison and Comment.
        New York: Edgar H. Wells; London: Charles J.
        Sawyer, Ltd.

63   Haight, Sherman P. "George Cruikshank: In His Vast
        Output Cruikshank Provided Recreation, a

Broadening Education and Infinite Amusement."
The Publisher's Weekly 114: 2059-63.

Brief biographical sketch.

64   Reid, Forrest. *Illustrators of the Sixties*.
      London: Faber and Gwyer.

Brief discussion of Tenniel, Millais, Keene,
Du Maurier, Fildes and others.

Appendix lists first editions of books illustrated by artists of the sixties.

65   Sadleir, Michael. *Trollope: A Bibliography. An
      Analysis of the History and Structure of the
      Works of Anthony Trollope, and a general
      survey of the effect of original publishing
      conditions on a book's subsequent rarity.*
      London: Constable & Co. "Addenda and corri-
      genda" issued in 1934. See *TLS* (December 6,
      1934): 880. Reprinted 1964 by Dawsons,
      London. See 145.

Valuable information about Trollope's
illustrators.

1929

66   Lehmann-Haupt, C. F. "New Facts Concerning *Edwin
      Drood.*" *The Dickensian* 25: 165-75.

Charles Collins, the illustrator originally
chosen for *The Mystery of Edwin Drood,* produced, in
addition to the cover-design, sketches for early numbers of the novel. He was forced by ill-health to
withdraw from the collaboration.

The published cover was redrawn by Luke Fildes.

See Cardwell, 276.

67   Thackeray, William Makepeace. *The Thackeray Alpha-*
          bet. Written and Illustrated by William
          Makepeace Thackeray. London: John Murray.

          First edition of a Thackeray work composed and
      illustrated about 1833.

68   Winterich, John T. "George Du Maurier and *Trilby.*"
          Books and the Man. New York: Greenberg,
          102-22.

          "Never in English or any other literature has
      there been exhibited such a happy marriage of
      talents as Du Maurier's. Author-illustrators and
      illustrator-authors were no fresh phenomenon before
      Du Maurier's day (the name of Thackeray occurs
      instantly and inevitably), but never before or since
      has there lived a novelist who could delineate his
      characters so exactly as he wished them to appear
      to himself and to his readers."

                            1930

69   Field, William. *John Leech On My Shelves.* Private-
          ly printed.

70   Griffin, Margaret S. "Cruikshank." *Golden Book* 12
          (December): 58-61.

          Popular biographical sketch.

71   Ley, J. W. T. "Dickens and Surtees." *The Dickensian*
          27: 66-68.

          The idea for *The Pickwick Papers* was Dickens'
      own. Refutes idea that the idea for the book came
      to Dickens from Surtees' *Jorrock's Jaunts and
      Jollities* through Seymour.

72   Reid, Forrest. "Charles Keene, Illustrator."
          Print Collector's Quarterly 17: 23-47.

      Keene as novel illustrator.

73   Rümann, Arthur. *Das Illustrierte Buch des XIX
          Jahrhunderts in England, Frankreich und
          Deutschland, 1790-1860.* Leipzig: Im Insel-Verlag.

      A study of the illustrated books of Cruikshank,
      Gilbert, Doyle, Meadows and Browne.

                        1931

74   Spielmann, M. H. and Walter Jerrold. *Hugh Thomson:
          His Art, His Letters, His Humour and His Charm.*
          London: A. & C. Black.

      Biography of the late Victorian illustrator.

75   Tidy, Gordon. *A Little about Leech.*   London:
          Constable.

      Brief appreciation.

                        1932

76   Darton, F. J. Harvey. *Children's Books in England:
          Five Centuries of Social Life.* Cambridge:
          Cambridge University Press.

      Includes survey of illustrated children's books
      of the Victorian period.

77   Ley, J. W. T.   "Fair Play for Buss." *The Dickensian*
          28: 258-64.

          It is a mistake to judge the artistic talents
      of Robert William Buss solely on his failure as an
      illustrator for Dickens' *The Pickwick Papers.*

          "Buss was not dismissed because his illustra-
      tions as such were unsatisfactory. These had been
      approved by the publishers, and some say by the
      author, so that no question of his ability as an
      illustrator arose. The trouble lay solely in the
      etching, which was a more or less mechanical process
      for which practice alone was necessary."

                              1933

78   Hatton, Thomas, and Arthur H. Cleaver. *A Biblio-*
          graphy of The Periodical Works of Charles
          Dickens: Bibliographical Analytical and
          Statistical. London: Chapman & Hall.

79   Strange, E. H.   "The Original Plates in *Nicholas*
          Nickleby." *The Dickensian* 29: 227-28.

          Phiz's plates for Dickens' *Nicholas Nickleby*
      "express the essential Dickens philosophy that human
      life is in general, in spite of its horrors and
      cruelties, in public a jolly hubbub and in private
      extremely cosy. They are forcible and full of life
      and movement and amusing detail."

          "Including two portraits there were apparently
      one hundred and twenty-six varieties of the forty
      plates....All variations are in comparatively minute
      and insignificant details."

80   Watson, Frederick. *Robert Smith Surtees. A Critical*
          Study. London: G. G. Harrap.

                              .

1934

81   Balston, Thomas. "English Book Illustrations, 1880-
          1900." *New Paths in Book Collecting. Essays
          by Various Hands.* Ed. John Carter. London:
          Constable, 163-90.

          An outline of the period for collectors. In-
      cludes a checklist of illustrated books.

82   Balston, Thomas. "Illustrated Series of the 'Nine-
          ties.'" *Book-Collector's Quarterly* 11 (July-
          September): 33-56; 14 (April-June): 35-53.

          Publisher's series of illustrated novels pub-
      lished in the 1890s described.

83   Lindsay, Lionel. *Charles Keene. The Artists'
          Artist.* London: R. & D. Colnaghi. Not seen.

84   Miller, W. and E. H. Strange. "The Original
          Pickwick Papers, The Collation of a Perfect
          First Edition." *The Dickensian* 29: 303-09;
          30: 31-37, 121-24, 177-80, 249-59; 31: 35-40;
          31 (1935): 95-99, 219-22, 284-86.

          An attempt to "lay down the requirements of a
      perfect copy" of Dickens' *The Pickwick Papers.* In-
      cludes comparison of Seymour and Phiz plates and
      detailed commentary on all the illustrations.

1935

85   Lemann, Bernard. "English Caricature." *American
          Magazine of Art* 28: 548-55.

          Brief mention of Cruikshank, Seymour, Leech and
      Thackeray.

23

86   Rais, Françoise. "Charles Dickens et les illus-
         trateurs de son oeuvre." *Arts et Métiers
         Graphiques* (October 15):   15-22.

87   Stonehouse, J. H., ed. *Catalogue of the Library of
         Charles Dickens from Gadshill reprinted from
         Sotheran's 'Price Current of Literature' Nos.
         CLXXIV and CLXXV; Catalogue of His Pictures and
         Objects of Art sold by Messrs. Christie, Manson
         & Woods, July 9, 1870; Catalogue of the Library
         of W. M. Thackeray sold by Messrs. Christie,
         Manson & Woods March 18, 1864 and Relics From
         His Library Comprising Books Enriched With His
         Characteristic Drawings reprinted from
         Sotheran's 'Price Current of Literature' No.
         CLXXVII.* London: Piccadilly Foundation Press.

1936

88   "Buss's *Pickwick* Pictures: An Important Letter."
         The Dickensian 32:   101-04.

         Letter from R. W. Buss to John Forster protest-
      ing a slighting reference to Buss's failure as an
      illustrator for Dickens' *The Pickwick Papers*.

89   "Dickens's Instructions to 'Phiz' for the *Pickwick*
         Illustrations." *The Dickensian* 32:   266-68,
         283.

         Four of the original drawings by "Phiz" for *The
      Pickwick Papers* are reproduced complete with
      Dickens's instructions for their improvement.

90   Dexter, Walter and J. W. T. Ley. *The Origin of
         Pickwick: New Facts Now First Published in the
         Year of the Centenary.* London: Chapman and
         Hall.

Account of the composition of *The Pickwick Papers* detailing Dickens' collaboration with Robert Seymour, R. W. Buss and H. K. Browne. The authors defend R. W. Buss from negative comments made by John Forster, Dickens' biographer, and others.

91   Miller, William and E. H. Strange. *A Centenary Bibliography of 'The Pickwick Papers.'* London: Argonaut.

92   Summers, Montague. "The Illustrations of the 'Gothick' Novels." *The Connoisseur* 98: 266-71.

Illustrations to late eighteenth- and early nineteenth-century gothic fiction. Mention of Cruikshank and Gilbert illustrations for W. H. Ainsworth's *Rookwood.*

1937

93   "Letters to John Leech Now First Printed." *The Dickensian* 34: 3-13; 34 (1938): 101-09, 175-83, 225-31; 35 (1938): 37-44.

Letters from Dickens to the illustrator John Leech discussing Leech's illustrations for *A Christmas Carol, The Chimes, The Cricket on the Hearth* and *The Battle of Life.*

94   "*Prospectus*: The Nonesuch Dickens." *Nonesuch Dickensiana: Retrospectus and Prospectus: The Nonesuch Dickens.* Bloomsbury: The Nonesuch Press, 123-30.

Description of the Nonesuch Press edition of Dickens "embellished with more than eight hundred illustrations...*carefully printed from the original plates and blocks.*"

95   *"Retrospectus:* Editions of Dickens's Works."
      Nonesuch Dickensiana: Retrospectus and
      Prospectus: The Nonesuch Dickens. Bloomsbury:
      The Nonesuch Press, 79-122.

      Important Dickens editions of the past reviewed
      through the exhibition of specimen pages.

96   Feipel, Louis N. "The American Issues of 'Trilby.'"
      Colophon ns II, 4:   537-49.

      Variants in the American issues of Du Maurier's
      illustrated novel.

97   Gossop, R. P. *Book Illustration: A Review of the*
      Art as it is To-day. With a foreword by Hugh
      R. Dent. The seventh Dent Memorial Lecture
      delivered at the London School of Printing on
      1st October 1937. New York: Oxford University
      Press.

      Brief comment on the techniques and recent
      history of book illustration.

98   Hatton, Thomas. "A Bibliographical List of the
      Original Illustrations to the Works of Charles
      Dickens Being Those Made Under his Supervision."
      Nonesuch Dickensiana: Retrospectus and
      Prospectus: The Nonesuch Dickens. Bloomsbury:
      The Nonesuch Press, 53-78.

      "A Census of all the illustrations to the Works
      of Charles Dickens which were made during his
      lifetime."

99   Millar, C. C. Hoyer. *George du Maurier and Others.*
      London: Cassell & Co.

100   Sitwell, Sacheverell. *Narrative Pictures: A Survey*
      of English Genre and its Painters. Notes on

the illustrations by Michael Sevier. London:
Batsford.

Discussion of Cruikshank oil paintings.

101 Waugh, Arthur. "Charles Dickens and His Illustra-
        tors." *Nonesuch Dickensiana: Retrospectus and
        Prospectus: The Nonesuch Dickens.* Bloomsbury:
        The Nonesuch Press, 7-52.

"The original Dickens illustrations are an
integral part of the Dickens stories, almost as
closely allied with the author's appeal as the text
itself."

Description of the original plates to be used
in the production of the Nonesuch Dickens.

Chronological account of Dickens' collaboration
with his illustrators.

                              1938

102 Dexter, Walter. "Author and Artist: The Claims of
        George Cruikshank Definitely Refuted After One
        Hundred Years and the Discovery of a New Work
        by Dickens." *The Dickensian* 34: 97-100.
        Correction on page 214 of the same volume.

New letters from Dickens to Cruikshank disprove
Cruikshank's statement that he had suggested the
original idea of the story of *Oliver Twist.*

103 Dexter, Walter, ed. *Charles Dickens to John Leech.
        Correspondence Now First Published.* London:
        Walter Dexter.

104 Dexter, Walter, ed. *The Letters of Charles Dickens.*
        The Nonesuch Dickens. 3 vols. Bloomsbury:
        Nonesuch Press.

                              27

105   Reitlinger, Henry. *From Hogarth to Keene: With 87*
      Reproductions of Black and White Drawings by
      English Story-Telling Artists and Illustrators.
      London: Methuen.

106   Sitwell, Sacheverell. "Some Aspects of National
      Genius: George Cruikshank." *Trio: Disserta-*
      tions on Some Aspects of National Genius. By
      Osbert, Edith and Sacheverell Sitwell. De-
      livered as the Northcliffe Lectures at the
      University of London in 1937. London:
      Macmillan, 219-48.

      "It is not an exaggeration to say that the
      whole of Dickens has become visible to us through
      the eyes of Cruikshank. His interpretation of
      Oliver Twist, and of the *Sketches by Boz,* was only
      followed in feeble imitation by 'Phiz' and others
      all through the works of Dickens."

      The essay focuses on plates in the *Comic*
      Almanack.

107   Weitenkampf, Frank. *The Illustrated Book.*
      Cambridge, Mass.: Harvard University Press.

      Brief treatment of English and American novel
      illustration.

                          1940

108   Bechtel, Edwin De T. "Illustrated Books of the
      Sixties: A Reminder of a Great Period in
      Illustration." *Print* 1 (June): 81-89. Re-
      printed in the Thirtieth Anniversary issue of
      Print 23 (May, 1969): 20-23.

      Works illustrated in the 1860s by Tenniel,
      Gilbert, Millais and Houghton discussed.

109   Lanoire, Maurice. "Un Anglo-Francais, Georges Du
           Maurier." *Revue de Paris* (March 15): 263-81.

110   Lehmann-Haupt, Hellmut. "English Illustrators in
           the Collection of George Arents." *Colophon*
           New Graphic Series I, 4: 23-46.

      Includes works by Cruikshank, Browne, Leech,
   Thackeray, Millais and Du Maurier.

111   Parrish, M. L. *Catalogue of an Exhibition of the
           Works of William Makepeace Thackeray Together
           with Books Articles and Catalogues Referring
           to Thackeray Held at the Library Co. of
           Philadelphia Ridgway Branch, May 14th to 28th,
           1940.* Philadelphia, Pa.: Privately printed.

112   R.   "Thackeray's Drawings." *Notes and Queries* 178:
           82. See also J. Ardagh, 178:   179; Edward
           Heron-Allen, 178:   231-32; St. Vincent
           Troubridge, 180:   269.

113   Roe, F. Gordon. "Old Christmas Books." *The
           Connoisseur* 106:   244-48, 266.

      Illustrations in Victorian Christmas books.

114   Sloan, John. "In Praise of Thackeray's Pictures."
           Vanity Fair. By William Makepeace Thackeray.
           New York: Heritage Press, xiii.

      Vanity Fair "with the illustrations by
   Thackeray himself is the best example of book illustration ever printed."

1941

115   McKenzie, Gordon. "Dickens and Daumier." *Studies
         in the Comic*. University of California
         Publications in English. Vol. 8:   273-98.

      Dickens and Daumier as caricaturists.

1942

116   Hill, Thomas W. [Kentley Bromhill, pseud.] "Phiz's
         Illustrations to *Dombey and Son*." *The
         Dickensian* 38:   219-21, 227; 39:   48-51, 57-60.

      Phiz's illustrations for *Dombey and Son* reach
      the "high-water mark" of his work as a draughtsman.

      "In the case of Dickens and Browne we are not
      getting the artist's conception only. We are pre-
      sented with the writer's conception, and the artist
      is only the medium for presenting pictorially what
      the novelist has conceived in literary form. That
      is why Boz and Phiz are inseparable. Never did a
      draughtsman study so earnestly the text he had to
      illustrate, and never did a draughtsman realize so
      successfully the characters and incidents as they
      had formed themselves in the mind of the author."

      Commentary on the cover, the frontispiece, the
      title vignette and on all the plates.

117   Low, David. *British cartoonists, Caricaturists, and
         Comic artists*. London: William Collins.

      Brief mention of novel illustration.

118   Roe, F. Gordon. "Talking of Dombey." *The
         Connoisseur* 109:   177-78.

H. K. Browne's wrapper illustration to *Dombey and Son* and its similarity to Browne's engraved title for Thomas Miller's *Godfrey Malvern* (1843).

119 Simon, Howard. *500 Years of Art in Illustration: From Albrecht Durer to Rockwell Kent.* Cleveland: World Publishing.

Brief popular introduction to the work of Cruikshank, Browne, Leech, Tenniel and others.

1943

120 "A New Dickens Bibliography." *The Dickensian* 39: 99-101, 149-53, 173-75; 40: 36-37; 40 (1944): 76-78, 143-45.

Guide to Dickens first editions.

121 Gerould, Gordon Hall. "Cruikshank's Literary Background." *The Princeton University Library Chronicle* 4: 62-64.

Sketch of the "literary climate" during Cruikshank's early years.

122 Grubb, Gerald Giles. "A Hogarth Influence on Dickens." *The Dickensian* 39: 144-45.

"Hogarth's painting entitled 'The Bathos' exerted direct influence on Dickens's mind, and through him, on the art of his illustrator, George Cattermole" in *Master Humphrey's Clock*.

123 Hill, Thomas W. [Kentley Bromhill, pseud.] "Phiz's Illustrations to *David Copperfield*." *The Dickensian* 40: 47-50; 40 (1944): 83-86.

Commentary on the cover and on all the plates
prepared by H. K. Browne for Dickens' novel.

124   Mather, Frank Jewett, Jr.   "George Cruikshank,
         artist." *The Princeton University Library
         Chronicle* 4:   53-61.

      Brief outline of Cruikshank's career.

      "Enough if I have dispelled the myth of George
      Cruikshank as a faithful recorder of the humors of
      English low life, and have succeeded in enthroning
      him as the king of whimsey, at times of graphic
      melodrama, and always as the master of fairy and
      goblin lore."

125   Price, Frances.   "'Phiz' and the Two Mrs. Meynells."
         Notes and Queries 184:   213-14.

      Quotations from articles and a book mentioning
      H. K. Browne.

126   Weitenkampf, Frank.   "Influences and Trends in
         Nineteenth-Century Illustration." *Bookmen's
         Holiday: Notes and Studies Written and
         Gathered in Tribute to Harry Miller Lydenberg.*
         New York: New York Public Library, 345-50.

      Mechanical techniques of book illustration in
      the Victorian period.

1944

127   Hill, Thomas W.   [Kentley Bromhill, pseud.]   "Phiz's
         Illustrations to *Bleak House.*" *The Dickensian*
         40:   146-50, 192-95.

      "Hablot K. Browne's illustrations to *Bleak
      House* maintain the high level of excellence that he
      had attained in his plates to *Dombey and Son.* After

a slight falling-off in his work for *David Copperfield*, he apparently threw himself heart and soul into the plot of *Bleak House* as it developed, building up the tragic scenes to their climax, and relieving his feelings by dealing with the humorous episodes in the most lighthearted way. Nearly all the plates exhibit careful craftsmanship, and in very few indeed is there evidence of exaggeration or caricature."

Commentary on monthly wrapper cover design, on the frontispiece, the title vignette and on all the plates.

128   Hubbard, Eric Hesketh. *Some Victorian Draughtsmen.*
      Cambridge: Cambridge University Press.

129   Orwell, George. "Oysters and Brown Stout." *Tribune*
      (December 22). Reprinted in *The Collected Essays, Journalism and Letters of George Orwell*. Ed. Sonia Orwell and Ian Angus. 4 vols. London: Secher & Warburg, vol. 3, 229-306.

Thackeray was "primarily a journalist, a writer of fragments, and his most characteristic work is not fully separable from the illustrations."

130   Quennell, Peter. "A Note on Richard Doyle." *The Cornhill* 161: 224, 275.

Reproductions of pages from the illustrated correspondence of Doyle.

Doyle, Edward Lear and Lewis Carroll were "representatives of an ancient tradition. The love of the fantastic is as old and as deep-rooted as the love of art itself; always, bordering the world of poetic imagination, there has existed another world-- a reflection, no doubt, of the duskier side of every human mind and of the less rational human impulses--where the satyr crashes through the undergrowth and the were-wolf howls: where the sweating goblin labours to earn his cream-bowl and the

warlock's animal familiar comes scuffling down the
chimney. It is the playground of Bosch and
Breughel, the setting of Goya's extravaganzas and
of Callot's darkness visions. Sometimes it wears a
terrible aspect: sometimes an air of rabelaisian
burlesque. Victorian artists were fully conscious
of the spell it exercised: they too loved the
fantastic and cultivated the grotesque: but their
interpretation was coloured by the Victorian temper-
ament: and the wonderlands and fairylands they
created are all the stranger and more mysterious
because so many uncouth and disturbing presences
have been diligently excluded--because the nightmare
has been broken and saddled and is trotted up as a
quiet saddle-horse for innocent family outings."

131   Richardson, Louisa E. "Centenary of a Notable
         Artist." *Journal of the Royal Society of Arts*
         42 (February 4): 141-42.

      Brief comment on the work of E. L. Sambourne,
   illustrator for *Punch* and for Kingsley's *Water-
   Babies* (1885).

                        1945

132   Booth, Bradford A. "The Parrish Trollope Collection."
         Nineteenth-Century Fiction 1 (Summer): 11-19.

      Brief description of collection now at
   Princeton University.

133   Etherington, J. R. M. "R. D. Blackmore and his
         Illustrators." *Notes and Queries* 188: 119-21.

      Correspondence between the novelist R. D.
   Blackmore and his illustrators.

                        34

134 Heintzelman, Arthur W. "Illustrations to Dickens's
        work by 'Kyd.'" *More Books. The Bulletin of
        The Boston Public Library* 20: 358-59.

        Watercolors of Dickens' characters by "Kyd,"
     J. Clayton Clark.

135 Millican, John N. B. "Dickens Illustrations." *TLS*
        (April 7): 163. See Douglas G. Browne,
        A. G. Schaw-Milles, Eric J. Layton, *TLS* (April
        28): 199; Oliver Millar and R. L. Hayne, *TLS*
        (May 5): 211; Herbert Brown, C. G. Henderson,
        Mat. C. Byrne, *TLS* (May 12): 223; Shane
        Leslie, *TLS* (May 19): 235.

        Controversy over the worth of the illustrations
     to Dickens' novels.

136 Millican, John N. B. "'Phiz' Without Sparkle." *The
        Dickensian* 41: 193-96.

        "A most pleasing post-war reform would be the
     complete elimination of the illustrations by Hablot
     K. Browne (and Cruikshank as well, for that matter)
     from new editions of Dickens's works. It is remark-
     able how these drawings have clung so tenaciously
     to the master of English novelists, a permanent
     burden on his shoulders, and indeed been regarded by
     many to be quite inseparable from him; for not one
     jot can be added by them to his great reputation or
     to his well-deserved popularity in all parts of the
     world. But reproductions keep reappearing just as
     if they were an essential feature of the stories
     they claim to embellish and not merely a species of
     literary barnacle, void alike of serious intrinsic
     merit and aesthetic beauty."

        See a reply, 139.

137 Thackeray, William Makepeace. *The Letters and Pri-
        vate Papers of William Makepeace Thackeray.*
        Ed. Gordon N. Ray. 4 vols. Cambridge, Mass.:
        Harvard University Press. 1945-1946.

Correspondence with and about illustrators;
Thackeray's comments on his own novel illustrations.

138   Weitenkampf, Frank. "Illustrators in Masquerade;
       a Short Chapter in Dickens Bibliography."
       Bulletin of the New York Public Library 49:
       423-26.

       Misstatements involving illustrators of the
       title pages of American editions of Dickens.

139   Yarre, d'A. P. "Dickens without Phiz?" *The
       Dickensian* 42: 32-34.

       A reply to 136.

       "We can only infer that Dickens, in common with
       other novelists of his time, considered illustra-
       tions essential and that he found Phiz his ideal
       illustrator, and that if that be the case we have no
       right to question his judgment."

1946

140   Taylor, Robert H. "The Trollope Collection."
       Princeton University Library Chronicle 8:
       33-37.

1947

141   Cameron, William Ross. *David Copperfield in Copper-
       plate: 46 Illustrations for the Famous Dickens
       Novel Augmented by Interpretative Short Passages
       taken from the Original Text.* Los Angeles:
       Wayne L. McNaughton. Not seen.

142   Gordan, John D.   "William Makepeace Thackeray:
          1811-1863." *Bulletin of the New York Public
          Library* 51:   259-96.

      Catalogue of an exhibition of first editions,
manuscripts, letters and drawings from the Berg
Collection.

143   Holbrook, John Pinckney.   "A Cruikshank Catalogue
          Raisonné: Notes and Corrections to Albert M.
          Cohn's *George Cruikshank, A Catalogue
          Raisonné..."* The Papers of the Bibliographical
          Society of America* 41:   144-47.

      The notes and corrections to his 1924 catalogue
are Cohn's own. See 48.

144   Hudson, Derek.   *Charles Keene*.   London: Pleiades
          Art Books.

145   Jabez-Smith, A. R.   "Luke Fildes."   *TLS* (March 22):
          127. See D. Pepys Whiteley and Michael Sadleir,
          TLS (April 5):   157; Luke V. Fildes, Michael
          Sadleir, H. F. Finberg and H. P. Garwood, *TLS*
          (April 19): 183; C. T. Smith, *TLS* (May 3):
          211; J. W. Kirby, *TLS* (May 17): 239.

      Luke Fildes was not the illustrator of *The Way
We Live Now* as Sadleir claimed in 65.

146   James, Philip.   *English Book Illustration 1800-1900*.
          London: King Penguin Books.

      Brief overview of nineteenth-century book
illustration with mention of Cruikshank, Leech,
Doyle, Keene, Millais, Tenniel and others.

147   Mahoney, Bertha E., Louise P. Latimer, and Beulah
          Folmsbee, compilers. *Illustrators of Children's
          Books 1744-1945*. Boston: Horn Book Inc.

A collection of essays on children's book
illustration. Includes bibliographies of illustrators and authors of children's books.

See in particular Jacqueline Overton, "Illustrators of the Nineteenth Century in England" (25-
86), and Helen Gentry, "Graphic Processes in
Children's Books" (161-72).

148 Thackeray, William Makepeace. *The Rose and the
        Ring*. Reproduced in facsimile from the
        Author's original illustrated manuscript in the
        Pierpont Morgan Library. Introduction by
        Gordon N. Ray. New York: The Pierpont Morgan
        Library.

149 Weitenkampf, Frank. "Thackeray, Illustrator."
        Bulletin of the New York Public Library 51:
        640-43.

Thackeray's practice of art "is after all a
significant phase of his nature and of his career.
And we would not do without it, even though we turn
to his novels for the masterly language, the deep
insight, which it was not given to him to express
with the pencil."

1948

150 "Trilby Re-appears." *TLS* (April 3): 191.

Commentary on Du Maurier's illustrated novels
Trilby, Peter Ibbetson and *The Martians*.

151 Friedman, Albert B. "English Illustrators of the
        1860's." *More Books. The Bulletin of the
        Boston Public Library* 23: 372-80.

152 Hambourg, Daria. *Richard Doyle: His Life and Work*.
        English Masters of Black-and-White. London:
        Art and Technics.

        "No artist knew better how to convey the vital
     and exhilarating crowd and the achievements of the
     mature Richard in this respect can be traced back to
     his early works. In fact, all his later styles may
     be discerned in these works--the decorative fancy
     and ingenious lettering, the nice sense of unity
     between text and design, the comical puppets and
     the handling of groups which gave their unified
     character without losing sight of individual peculi-
     arities. It may even be held, in the light of his
     youthful performance, that Doyle's artistic develop-
     ment matured at fifteen and that he never subsequent-
     ly improved upon it."

        "After his secession from *Punch*, Doyle became
     mainly an illustrator, producing among other works
     the drawings for Thackeray's *The Newcomes* (1854 and
     1855). It may be doubted whether Doyle ever found a
     writer whose sense of humour more exactly matched
     his own, and the Newcome volumes abound in brilliant
     examples of their joint wit."

        Includes a listing of works illustrated by
     Doyle.

153 McLean, Ruari. *George Cruikshank: His Life and
        Work as a Book Illustrator*. English Masters of
        Black-and-White. London: Art and Technics.

        Traces Cruikshank's career as novel illustrator,
     focusing on his collaboration with Dickens and
     Ainsworth.

        "It was not idly that Ruskin compared his skill
     as an etcher with that of Rembrandt. Nearly every
     etched illustration by Cruikshank is a careful and
     studied picture, every part of which is related to
     the intended effects of the whole, with exquisite
     shading and a masterly representation of every depth
     of shadow."

        "His etching technique was superb: but perhaps
     his greatest gift was his sense of the dramatic. He

might have been a successful illustrator for Jane
Austen--the vignettes in *The Beauties of Washington
Irving*, for example, show that--but he was at his
best where drama, mystery, horror, or excitement
were required. Probably no other illustrator has
ever made so many pictures that haunt the memory
for their own sakes, even if the context is unknown
or forgotten."

Includes a "Select List" of books illustrated
by Cruikshank.

154   Sarzano, Frances. *Sir John Tenniel*. English
         Masters of Black-and-White. London: Art and
         Technics.

Includes brief account of Tenniel as book
illustrator. "Tenniel was a conscientious illustrator who studied his texts carefully."

"Tenniel's illustrations to Shirley Brook's two
novels, *The Silver Cord* (serialized in *Once a Week,*
1860-1) and *The Gordian Knot* (1860), include some
very pleasing drawings--attractive enough to make
one regret that he illustrated so few novels and so
many ballads and Norse legends."

"There have been many better drawings for books
than those done by Tenniel in the *Alices* but better
illustrations do not exist. Carroll's two books not
only exact from the artist every ability he possesses,
they turn his limitations equally to account. Elsewhere, Tenniel's precise, matter-of-fact line seems
sometimes insensitive; as a container for Carroll's
explicit imagination, it is this very quality of
flat statement which makes the drawing ideal. *Alice*
could not be illustrated with fairy-tale gossamers;
its characters are too trenchant with reality--
though it is reality encountered on uncustomary
planes. From Tenniel's exact pencil the creatures
of Wonderland spring into definition: one after
another, they are seen with the dreamer's precise
vision and overwhelming certitude."

Includes a listing of works illustrated by
Tenniel.

155   Smith, Janet Adam. *Children's Illustrated Books*.
          London: Collins.

          Brief history of children's book illustration.
      Includes mention of Cruikshank, Thackeray, Tenniel,
      Arthur Hughes, Walter Crane and others.

156   Weitenkampf, Frank. "What the Early Illustrators
          Did to Dickens." *American Collector* 17
          (September): 9-11. Not seen.

157   Whiteley, Derek Pepys. *George Du Maurier: His Life
          and Work*. English Masters of Black-and-White.
          London: Art and Technics.

          Account of Du Maurier as illustrator of his own
      novels (*Peter Ibbetson, The Martian,* and *Trilby*),
      and of the novels of Elizabeth Gaskell and others.

          Du Maurier's best known work, which appeared in
      Punch from 1860 to 1896, gives "a fascinating
      panorama of the Victorian upper and middle class
      scene. Less accessible are examples of his early
      work, buried in long-forgotten and now rarely found
      periodicals--drawings which, it is suggested,
      entitle George Du Maurier to be ranked among the
      greatest masters of black-and-white who flourished
      in that brief golden decade--'The 'Sixties.'"

          Includes a listing of books illustrated by Du
      Maurier.

                        1950

158   Fitzgerald, P. M. "Notes on the Fairy Pictures of
          Richard Doyle." *World Review* (December):
          64-67.

159   Hopkins, Annette B. "A Uniquely Illustrated
          'Cranford.'" *Nineteenth-Century Fiction* 4:
          299-314.

An American edition of Mrs. Gaskell's *Cranford* illustrated with original water colors by W. H. Drake.

See Lauterbach, 169.

160 Rose, June. *The Drawings of John Leech*. English
     Masters of Black-and-White. London:
     Art and Technics. Not seen.

1951

161 Bland, David. *The Illustration of Books*. London:
     Faber and Faber, 11-18, 60-79. Third, enlarged
     edition, 1962.

     Brief mention of novel illustration.

162 Du Maurier, Daphne, ed. *The Young George Du Maurier:*
     A Selection of His Letters, 1860-67. With a
     biographical index by Derek Pepys Whiteley.
     London: Davies.

163 Sadleir, Michael. *XIX Century Fiction: A Biblio-*
     graphical Record Based on His Own Collection by
     Michael Sadleir. 2 vols. Cambridge: Cambridge
     University Press.

1952

164 Coôper, Leonard. *R. S. Surtees*. London: Arthur
     Barker.

     Biography and survey of his work.

165   Johnson, Edgar. *Charles Dickens: His Tragedy and Triumph*. 2 vols. Boston: Little, Brown.

This definitive biography contains information on Dickens' collaboration with his illustrators.

166   Ray, Gordon N. "The Importance of Original Editions." *Nineteenth-Century English Books: Some Problems in Bibliography*. Third Annual Windsor Lectures in Librarianship. Includes addresses by Carl J. Weber and John Carter. Urbana: University of Illinois Press.

1953

167   Gralapp, Leland Wilson. "Images of the Child Cult in Mid-Victorian Book Illustration." *Dissertation Abstracts* 13: 1147-48. State University of Iowa.

"Imagery revolving around the child is extremely pervasive in the visual and literary arts of the Victorian Period."

In book illustration, "the child-image tends to appear via four relatively distinct figurations (deriving from the Pastoral Tradition, transformed and transmitted by artists and poets of the Romanticist persuasion). In tracing the line of development from Joshua Reynolds and his successors of the English Portrait School, through Landseer and the PRB, to illustrators of Kingsley, MacDonald, Carroll, and Lear, we observe an unbroken tradition in which the child-image occurs in association with animal-imagery (reflecting the idea of the particularly intimate and harmonious relationship which the child is believed to maintain with Nature, a concept expressed also in the work of the Lakists and their illustrators). Through a comparable succession of instances it is shown that, owing chiefly to this supposed relationship, the child also appears as seer; being thought to possess an 'instinctual wisdom' which is felt to be no longer available to the

'socially conditioned' and 'institutionalized'
adult. It is then similarly indicated that the
child (mainly through association with water-sym-
bolism) likewise makes its appearance as healer, as
agent of spiritual redemption and regeneration, also
by virtue of his supposed kinship with Nature.
Finally we note the occurrence of the child-image in
its figuration as hero (most frequently in parallels
with the *Anastasis*, myths of Perseus, Orpheus,
etc.)."

168   Grubb, Gerald G. "Charles Green, R. I." *Notes and
          Queries* 198: 499.

          Green's illustrations for Dickens' stories and
      novels.

169   Lauterbach, Edward S. "A Note on 'A Uniquely
          Illustrated "Cranford."'" *Nineteenth-Century
          Fiction* 8: 232-34.

          Corrects errors in Hopkins, 159.

170   Stevenson, Lionel. "The Elkins Collection,
          Philadelphia Free Library." *Victorian News
          Letter* 3 (April): 6.

171   Weitenkampf, Frank. "American Illustrators of
          Dickens." *The Boston Public Library Quarterly*
          5: 189-94.

1954

172   Tillotson, Geoffrey. *Thackeray the Novelist*.
          Cambridge: Cambridge University Press.

          Recurring symbols in the illustrations are
      analyzed.

173 Tooley, R. V. *English Books with Coloured Plates
        1790 to 1860: A Bibliographical Account of
        the most Important Books illustrated by
        English Artists in Colour Aquatint and Colour
        Lithography.* London: B. T. Batsford.

1955

174 Bland, David. *The Book. Number Four. A Biblio-
        graphy of Book Illustrations.* London: Pub-
        lished for The National Book League by the
        Cambridge University Press.

175 Ray, Gordon N. *Thackeray: The Uses of Adversity
        1811-1846.* New York: McGraw-Hill.

        First volume of the definitive biography. See
     187.

        Useful commentary on Thackeray as his own
     illustrator.

1956

176 Ashley, Robert P. "The Wilkie Collins Collection."
        The Princeton University Library Chronicle 17:
        81-84.

        Wilkie Collins first editions in the Parrish
     Collection at Princeton.

177 Johannsen, Albert. *Phiz: Illustrations From the
        Novels of Charles Dickens.* Chicago: University
        of Chicago Press.

        Reproductions of 516 plates by H. K. Browne
     from novels by Dickens.

178   Martin, Robert B.   "The Reade Collection."   *The
        Princeton University Library Chronicle* 17:
        77-80.

        Collection of Charles Reade first editions at
    Princeton in the Parrish Collection.

179   Metzdorf, Robert F.   "M. L. Parrish and William
        Makepeace Thackeray." *The Princeton University
        Library Chronicle* 17:   68-70.

        Description of Parrish Thackeray collection at
    Princeton.

180   Taylor, Robert H.   "The Singular Anomalies."   *The
        Princeton University Library Chronicle* 17:
        71-76.

        Important first editions in The Morris L.
    Parrish Collection of Victorian Novelists.

181   Wainwright, Alexander D.   "The Morris L. Parrish
        Collection of Victorian Novelists; A Summary
        Report and an Introduction." *The Princeton
        University Library Chronicle* 17:   59-67.

182   Weaver, Warren.   "The Parrish Collection of
        Carrolliana." *The Princeton University Library
        Chronicle* 17:   85-91.

        Lewis Carroll's writings in the Parrish Col-
    lection at Princeton.

1957

183   Butt, John and Kathleen Tillotson.   *Dickens at Work.*
        London: Methuen.

The examination of several of Dickens' novels, among them *Sketches By Boz, Pickwick Papers, Barnaby Rudge, Dombey and Son, David Copperfield, Bleak House, Hard Times* and *Little Dorrit,* "in the light of the conditions under which he wrote them."

Contains discussions of the collaboration between Dickens and his illustrators.

184 Dickson, Sarah Augusta. "The Arents Collection of Books in Parts and Associated Literature: A Brief Survey." *Bulletin of the New York Public Library* 61: 267-80. Reprinted in book form with a brief descriptive checklist in the same year by the New York Public Library.

185 Price, R. G. G. *A History of 'Punch.'* London: Collins.

Contains information and commentary on many novel illustrators who worked for *Punch.*

1958

186 Bland, David. *A History of Book Illustration: The Illuminated Manuscript and the Printed Book.* London: Faber & Faber, 242-76. Second revised edition 1969.

Brief mention of Victorian novel illustration.

187 Ray, Gordon N. *Thackeray: The Age of Wisdom.* New York: McGraw-Hill. See 175.

Second and concluding volume of the definitive biography.

Contains information on Thackeray as illustrator and on his collaboration with Richard Doyle and others.

188   Swenson, Paul B.   "Thackeray Drawings in the Print
          Department." *Boston Public Library Quarterly*
          10:   101-05.

          Description of twelve Thackeray drawings.

189   Tillotson, Kathleen.   "Seymour Illustrating Dickens
          in 1834." *The Dickensian* 54:   11-12.

          Over a year before they collaborated on *The
          Pickwick Papers,* Robert Seymour had, "though no
          doubt unwittingly," illustrated Dickens' short story
          "The Bloomsbury Christening."

                              1959

190   Stange, G. Robert.   "Reprints of Nineteenth-Century
          British Fiction." *College English* 21:   178-83.

                              1960

191   Dupee, F. W., ed. *The Selected Letters of Charles
          Dickens.*   Introduction by F. W. Dupee.   New
          York: Farrar, Straus and Cudahy.

          Correspondence with and about Dickens' illus-
          trators included.

192   Gardner, Martin, ed. *The Annotated Alice: Alice's
          Adventures in Wonderland & Through the Looking
          Glass.*   By Lewis Carroll.   New York: Clarkson
          N. Potter.   Revised edition, 1964.

          Includes John Tenniel's illustrations.

1961

193 Butt, John. "Dickens's Instructions for *Martin
     Chuzzlewit*, Plate XVIII." *A Review of English
     Literature* 2 (July): 49-50.

     Dickens' instructions and H. K. Browne's sketch
     for the plate reproduced.

194 Carr, Sister Mary Callista. *Catalogue of The
     Dickens Collection at the University of Texas.*
     Austin: Humanities Research Center, The
     University of Texas.

1962

195 Antal, Frederick. "Hogarth's Impact on English Art."
     Hogarth and His Place in European Art. London:
     Routledge & Kegan Paul, 175-95.

     Mention of Hogarth's influence on Victorian
     novel illustrators.

196 Gimbel, Richard. "An Exhibition of 150 Manuscripts,
     Illustrations and First Editions of Charles
     Dickens to Commemorate the 150th Anniversary of
     his Birth." *The Yale University Library
     Gazette* 37 (October): 46-93.

1963

197 Cahoon, Herbert. "The Author as Illustrator." *Book
     Illustration: Papers presented at the Third
     Rare Book Conference of the American Library
     Association in 1962.* Berlin: Gebr·Mann·Verlag,
     66-73.

Mention of Thackeray and Richard Doyle.

198   Evans, Joan. *TLS* (December 5): 1011. Letter
        inquiring about illustrations in *Vanity Fair*.
        See Joan Bryant's reply, *TLS* (December 12):
        1031.

199   McLean, Ruari.   *Victorian Book Design and Colour
        Printing*. New York: Oxford University Press.

      Information about technical aspects of book
    illustration.

1964

200   Ray, Gordon N. "Contemporary Collectors XVIII: A
        19th-Century Collection." *Book Collector* 13:
        33-44, 171-84.

      Nineteenth-century illustrated books including
    many novels in parts and in first editions.

1965

201   Chapell, Marian G. "The Man Who Drew for Dickens."
        Country Life 137: 1447-48.

      H. K. Browne.

202   Dickens, Charles. *The Letters of Charles Dickens.
        Volume One 1820-1839*. Ed. Madeline House and
        Graham Storey. The Pilgrim Edition. Oxford:
        The Clarendon Press.

203   Robb, Brian.   "George Cruikshank's Etchings for
          Oliver Twist." *The Listener* 74: 130-31.

          Cruikshank was "the illustrator *par excellence*
      of the early Victorian era."

204   Robb, Brian.   "Tenniel's Illustrations to the 'Alice'
          Books." *The Listener* 74: 310-11.

          "Carroll's text quite translated Tenniel, and
      his illustrations to the *Alice* books raise him to a
      creative height he never approached on his own....
      Tenniel's unique qualification lay, it seems, in
      his detachment as a recorder; in a dispassionate
      attitude to the irrational that triumphantly brings
      out the demonic logic of his author....Better illus-
      trations in the strict sense than Tenniel's to the
      Alice books do not exist."

205   Stevens, Joan.   "Thackeray's Vanity Fair." *Review
          of English Literature* 6: 19-38.

          "Thackeray's illustrations have an important
      part to play in his fiction, a part which we have
      failed to appreciate" because "few reprints are
      illustrated, and those that are do not respect the
      original plan."

206   Stoehr, Taylor. *Dickens: The Dreamer's Stance.*
          Ithaca, New York: Cornell University Press,
          252-87.

          Brief mention of the effect of the
      illustrations.

          "Dickens' novels do not need illustration, any
      more than Tennyson's poems require to be read in the
      Moxon edition, but that they are perfectly suited to
      illustration can hardly be disputed; and this
      suitability may be traced finally to the dreamer's
      stance which Dickens takes, and especially to his
      habit of 'seeing' all the visible aspects of a
      scene, his hypostatizing of such scenes, so that

they offer themselves to the imagination almost
cinematically, in tableaux and 'all-at-once.'"

1966

207 Hannah, Donald. "'The Author's Own Candles': The
        Significance of the Illustrations to *Vanity
        Fair.*" *Renaissance and Modern Essays Presented
        to Vivian de Sola Pinto in Celebration of His
        Seventieth Birthday.* Ed. G. R. Hibbard with
        George A. Ponichas and Allan Rodway. London:
        Routledge and Kegan Paul, 119-27.

        Thackeray's strong pictorial imagination "only
        functions with full effect in the context of the
        prose." "The illustrations tend to present us with
        an all too explicit representation of the action;
        and in comparison with the richness of implication
        and complexity of attitude which lie behind
        Thackeray's most sharply imagined verbal pictures,
        the illustrations themselves seem lacking in depth
        and almost one-dimension." The illustrations, far
        from making of Thackeray a "prose Blake," are simply
        "an accompaniment to the action rather than an
        integral part of it or an amplification of it."
        There is an essential element lacking in the illus-
        trations: "they comment upon the narrative, not
        upon the narrator." Only a small sketch of the
        puppet master sitting cross-legged, the illustration
        found on the cover of the monthly installments, and
        that used for the title-page of the first edition
        suggest Thackeray's "conception of his own relation-
        ship as narrator to the people of Vanity Fair."

208 Lister, Raymond. *Victorian Narrative Paintings.*
        London: Museum Press.

        Brief mention of novel illustration.

        "The illustration of novels and story books
        must have provided one source for the spectacular
        rise of the narrative picture from about 1820 to
        about 1860."

209 Steig, Michael. "Phiz's Marchioness." *Dickens*
         Studies 2: 141-46.

         "The status of Browne's illustrations [to *The
    Old Curiosity Shop*] as critical evidence is...com-
    parable to that of Dickens's original intention to
    reveal the Marchioness as the product of a sexual-
    demonic liaison. For both corroborate the fragmen-
    tary findings of several critics that the character
    is surrounded by an aura of sexuality, even though
    no overt evidence of this sexuality is present in
    the novel. Dickens's intention regarding the
    girl's parentage indicates that in his primary
    conception he endowed her with a heritage radically
    different from that of his other female characters--
    a heritage of sexual vitality, perverse though it be;
    and Browne's illustrations, which are interpretations
    by a contemporary and associate of the novelist, in
    their variety furnish further proof that to find
    sexual ambiguity in the Marchioness of the novel's
    text is neither over-imaginative nor anachronistic."

210 Todd, William B. "Dickens's *Battle of Life*. Round
         Six." *Book Collector* 15: 48-54.

         Variations in the engraved title for the
    Dickens work.

                              1967

211 Evans, Edmund. *The Reminiscences of Edmund Evans*.
         Ed. Ruari McLean. Oxford: Clarendon Press.

         Reminiscences of a wood engraver and color
    printer (1826-1905).

212 George, M. Dorothy. *Hogarth to Cruikshank: Social
         Change in Graphic Satire*. New York: Walker
         and Company.

         Valuable background for the study of Cruikshank.

213   Patten, Robert L.   "The Art of *Pickwick*'s Interpo-
          lated Tales." *ELH* 34:   349-66.

          H. K. Browne's frontispiece to *The Pickwick
      Papers* sheds light on the novel's design.

          "The frontispiece, illustrating the complex
      interweaving of story, play, and experience that
      the novel demonstrates, thereby also illustrates
      its aesthetic. With such indications of the role
      played by the tales in the novel, we must revise our
      assumption that Dickens used them merely as filler.
      A few may be out of key with the tone of the main
      narrative, or only marginally relevant to the novel's
      principal concerns. Nevertheless in *Pickwick* the
      twenty-four-year-old Dickens enriched the popular
      but limited form of serial fiction by developing a
      narrative of many dimensions: plot, sub-plots,
      interpolated tales, and emblematic illustrations;
      Pickwick's tales provide one important means of
      advancing and commenting on its central action--the
      education of all Pickwickians, fictional and real."

214   Patten, Robert L.   "'So Much Pains about One Chalk-
          Faced Kid': The Clarendon *Oliver Twist*."
          Dickens Studies 3: 160-68.

          Review of Kathleen Tillotson's edition of
      Oliver Twist.

          "*Oliver Twist* now stands as the most comprehen-
      sively edited novel in the English language."

          "The Clarendon edition is the first to repro-
      duce the twenty-four Cruikshank plates in their
      original state, as they appeared in *Bentley's* before
      being touched up and rebitten for 1846."

          Cruikshank's "plates of low-life are an inte-
      gral part of the total effect of the scenes they
      represent"; in addition, they reinforce the
      symbolism of the novel.

215   Peyrouton, N. C. "When Nast Drew Dickens: An
          Historical Note and Correction." *The
          Dickensian* 63: 154-55.

The American cartoon-caricaturist Thomas Nast as illustrator of Dickens.

216 Stevens, Joan. "'Woodcuts Dropped into the Text': The Illustrations in *The Old Curiosity Shop* and *Barnaby Rudge*." *Studies in Bibliography* 20: 113-33.

"The purpose of this article is to demonstrate the relevance to their exact placing of the illustrations set into the text in the first published form of *The Old Curiosity Shop* and *Barnaby Rudge*, and to examine Dickens's policy in subsequent reprints. It will be shown that the insets function significantly in narrative, characterisation and theme, that the resulting composite achievement is remarkable, and that subsequent publishing failure to honour Dickens's intentions has disastrously obliterated the pointed textual relevance which his illustrations were planned to have."

1968

217 Cohen, Jane Rabb. "Dickens and His Original Illustrators." Harvard University. Dissertation.

218 Fildes, L. V. *Luke Fildes, R. A. A Victorian Painter.* London: Michael Joseph.

Some commentary on Fildes as novel illustrator.

219 Hutton, Muriel. "Unfamiliar Libraries XIII: The George MacDonald Collection, Brander Library, Huntly." *The Book Collector* 17: 13-25.

Illustrated editions of MacDonald's work mentioned.

220   Steig, Michael. "The Iconography of the Hidden Face
          in *Bleak House*." *Dickens Studies* 4: 19-22.

      The cumulative effect of some of Browne's
      illustrations to *Bleak House* "is to reinforce
      strongly the connections that are barely implied in
      the novel between Lady Dedlock's original crime and
      Esther's disfiguring disease."

      "And thus the suggestion of both Mark Spilka
      and Taylor Stoehr that Esther's disease is, sym-
      bolically, a sexual one, spread from Hawdon's grave
      to Esther by Jo, is given an unexpected kind of
      support by the novel's illustrations. This is not
      to say that either Dickens or Browne had such an
      equation consciously in mind; it is to say, rather,
      that if one allows the possibility of subliminal
      meanings in a Victorian novel, then the fact that
      Browne, working of course under Dickens's watchful
      eye, uses the hidden face to represent both disgrace
      and disease, must be seen as supporting strongly the
      theory that the novel itself implies such an
      equation."

221   Vogler, Roger A.   "The Inimitable George Cruikshank
          1792-1878." *The Inimitable George Cruikshank:
          An Exhibition of Illustrated Books, Prints,
          Drawings and Manuscripts from the Collection
          of David Borowitz*. J. B. Speed Art Museum,
          Univ. of Louisville (October 12-November 15,
          1968): 1-17.

      Brief appreciation.

                              1969

222   Bentley, Nicolas. "Dickens and his Illustrators."
          Charles Dickens 1812-1870: A Centenary Volume.
          Ed. E. W. F. Tomlin. London: Weidenfeld and
          Nicolson, 205-27. See also "The Illustrators,"
          196-204.

      A shortened version of this article appeared in
      The Dickensian 65: 148-62.

"No author ever gave greater inspiration to an illustrator than Dickens. To the richness of his imagination were added personal encouragement and criticism, as well as detailed descriptions of scenes and characters."

"The artists who originally illustrated Dickens—and there were sixteen altogether—were mostly of a fairly pedestrian order, but two of them, Cruikshank and Phiz, may be said to have made distinctive contributions to the understanding and enjoyment of Dickens."

223 Cohen, Jane R. "'All-of-a Twist': The Relationship of George Cruikshank and Charles Dickens." *Harvard Library Bulletin* 17: 169-94, 320-42.

Detailed account of the collaboration of Dickens and Cruikshank.

224 Dickens, Charles. *The Letters of Charles Dickens. Volume Two 1840-1841.* Ed. Madeline House and Graham Storey. The Pilgrim Edition. Oxford: Clarendon Press.

225 Harvey, J. R. "The Concern of Serial Novelists with the Illustration of their Work in the Nineteenth Century, with Particular Reference to Dickens." Cambridge, England. Dissertation.

226 Ormond, Leonée. *George du Maurier.* London: Routledge & Kegan Paul.

Full-length biography of the artist.

227 Patten, Robert L. "Boz, Phiz and Pickwick in the Pound." *ELH* 36: 575-91.

A reading of "Mr. Pickwick in the Pound," Plate 16 in Part VII of *Pickwick Papers.*

In his designs Browne "was able iconographic-
ally to point up themes the text elaborated
linguistically."

"Recent criticism has...concentrated on
identifying Dickens' peculiar mode, so realistic in
details, yet so unrealistic--theatrical, or express-
ionist, or allegorical--in its totality. The
combination has much in common with what Fielding,
Lamb, and Hazlitt perceived to be Hogarth's style,
and the parallels were not lost on Victorian critics.
Our best definition of Dickens' mode, and the
critical context for discussing it, may therefore
come from a fuller understanding of the character
of Victorian parts publication, and our knowledge of
the contributions made by the illustrations and the
traditions from which they derive."

228   Steig, Michael. "Dickens, Hablot Browne, and the
         Tradition of English Caricature." *Criticism*
         11: 219-33.

"Browne's illustrations to Dickens' novels...
like the novels' texts themselves, display a development from an essentially caricatural style to a more
complex and realistic one, as well as a gradual
development of techniques for expressing a sweeping
vision of the dehumanization of man's world. And
although some of the same stylistic developments can
be traced in Browne's illustrations for such minor
novelists as Lever and Ainsworth, this does not
lessen their significance for our understanding of
Dickens' works. For although there is as much dif-
ference between the characters in the illustrations
to Lever's early *Harry Lorrequer* (1839) and those in
The Dodd Family Abroad (1854), as there is between
those in the early *Nicholas Nickleby* and the later
Little Dorrit, this development does not have any
parallels in Lever's works. Moreover, although the
dark plate becomes ubiquitous in Browne's work from
the late 1840's up to about 1860, it is frequently
used mechanically and to no particular purpose
(Lever's *Roland Cashel* is a particularly blatant
example), and there is no group of dark plates that
is so rigorously dehumanized as those in *Bleak House*.
And finally, although contextual allegorical details
occur in Browne's illustrations to other novelists,
nowhere are they so heavily concentrated as in the

novels of Dickens' middle period. One may reasonably infer that Browne was influenced most strongly
by the greatest, and certainly the most demanding
of his employers, but whatever the facts of influence it seems clear that we have in Dickens' novels
the most perfect example of the integrity of illustrations and text--in matters of broad artistic
vision as well as in specific details--short of
those cases, such as Blake, Thackeray or Edward
Lear, where the author and artist are one and the
same."

229 Steig, Michael. *"Dombey and Son*: Chapter XXXI,
      Plate 20." *English Language Notes* 7: 124-27.

      H. K. Browne's illustration clarifies a
confusing passage in the novel.

230 Steig, Michael. *"Martin Chuzzlewit*: Pinch and
      Pecksniff." *Studies in the Novel* 1: 181-88.

      H. K. Browne's frontispiece suggests the im-
portance of the character Tom Pinch in the novel.

231 Stevens, Joan. "A Roundabout Ride." *Victorian
      Studies* 13: 53-70.

      Details in the text and illustrations of
Thackeray's *Vanity Fair* can be better understood
by examining a paper Thackeray wrote for *Punch* in
1848.

232 Szladits, Lola L., and Harvey Simmonds. *Pen and
      Brush: The Author as Artist.* An Exhibition
      in the Berg Collection of English and American
      Literature. New York: New York Public Library.

1970

233   Cohen, Jane Rabb.   "Strained Relations: Charles
          Dickens and George Cattermole." *Dickens
          Studies Annual* 1:   81-92.

      An account of the personal relationship and
collaboration of Dickens and Cattermole.

234   Curran, Stuart.   "The Lost Paradises of *Martin
          Chuzzlewit*." *Nineteenth-Century Fiction* 25:
          51-67.

      "In his illustration of the climactic moment
of *Martin Chuzzlewit*, the next to last plate in the
novel, Hablot Browne ('Phiz') artfully crowns a
metaphorical structure that has persisted in the
novel from literally its first sentence.   Entitled
'Warm Reception of Mr. Pecksniff by his Venerable
Friend,' the plate shows Pecksniff, fallen to the
floor of Martin's study under the patriarch's
merciless beating, with the rest of the assembly
frozen in surprise and a flurry of books toppling in
the confusion.   Of the two volumes whose titles can
be read, the most prominent is *Paradise Lost*.   This
minor and easily-overlooked detail is not merely an
irony appropriate to the collapse of Pecksniff's
house of trick cards, but is the single explicit
reference in *Martin Chuzzlewit* to the myth that
underlies the entire novel."

235   Harvey, J. R. *Victorian Novelists and their Illus-
          trators*.   London: Sidgwick and Jackson.

      "The book is not chiefly about the personal
contacts of author and artist..., but about the
contact of their arts.   Previous approaches to the
subject have been heavily biographical, giving useful but piecemeal accounts of the personal relation-
ships of writers and artists, and little has been
said about the illustrator's *art* and the way it
works in the novel.   This is a pity, for it is here,
rather than in the personal interest, that the
distinction of the illustrated serials lies.   They

vindicate the view that text and picture *can* truly
work together. That view needs defending at the
present time because when one thinks of what illustration can do, one inevitably thinks chiefly in
terms of modern illustrations, and modern illustrations are not equipped to be integral parts of
the novel: there is so little common ground between
the things that matter most for the visual artist
and those that matter most for the writer. The
illustrations in the monthly parts had faults of
melodrama and cramped technique from which we are
emancipated, but they embody an economy of standards
different from that which prevails now, and one that
is worth preserving because it shows how illustrations, while retaining their integrity as visual
art, can extend the preoccupations of a novelist.
The illustrations of Cruikshank and Phiz were not
confined to the vivid suggestion of character and
mood; they could develop a novel's themes subtly,
delicately, and powerfully, and in essentially
visual terms. Their mannerisms are of the past and
the specific historical conditions that encouraged
them are not likely to recur, but their inheritance
and activity defines certain general conditions
which must hold for any true collaboration of
distinct arts, and a sense of their priorities
should be sustained for the light it sheds, should
there be in the future a question of novel and picture working as one."

     Includes chapters treating the origins of book
illustration in the English tradition, "Gillray to
Cruikshank: Graphic Satire and Illustration,"
"Bruegel to Dickens: Graphic Satire and the Novel,"
"'A Voice Concurrent or Prophetical': The Illus-
trated Novels of W. M. Thackeray," "Dickens and
Browne: *Pickwick Papers* to *Barnaby Rudge*," "Dickens
and Browne: *Martin Chuzzlewit* to *Bleak House*" and
"Illustration and the Mind's Eye."

236 Leavis, Q. D. "The Dickens Illustrations: Their Func-
         tion." *Dickens the Novelist*. By F. R. Leavis
         and Q. D. Leavis. London: Chatto & Windus,
         332-71.

     "The suitability of Cruikshank and 'Phiz' for
Dickens was not accidental; the principle of conver-
gence that novelist and artists seem to exhibit so
successfully is due to their all belonging to the

tradition of a visual-literary moralistic-satiric
art with its roots in Pope and Hogarth."

237   Marten, Harry Paul. "The Visual Imagination: A
        Study of the Artistic Relationship of Charles
        Dickens and William Hogarth." *Dissertation
        Abstracts International* 31: 6017A. University
        of California, Santa Barbara.

        "This study examines the correspondences be-
      tween Charles Dickens's novels and the engravings
      of William Hogarth. Such a study intends to provide
      assistance in the understanding of Dickens's achieve-
      ment. It may help the reader to comprehend the
      puzzling blend of reality, fantasy, symbolism,
      terror and comedy in the novels, and it casts light
      upon the nature of the formal structure of Dickens's
      work."

238   Patten, Robert L. "Portraits of Pott: Lord
        Brougham and *The Pickwick Papers*." *The
        Dickensian* 66: 205-24.

        Reviewing the problems encountered during the
      progress of Plate 14 for *Pickwick* VI, "Mrs Leo
      Hunter's Fancy dress déjeuné," "from its inception
      in August 1836 through to the duplicate etched for
      the one-volume edition issued in November 1837,
      sheds light on the nature of Browne's collaboration
      with Dickens, and illuminates *Pickwick*'s relation
      to a long tradition of graphic and literary satire."

239   Reed, John R. "Emblems in Victorian Literature."
        Hartford Studies in Literature 2: 19-39.

        "My purpose is to suggest that in order to read
      the literature of the Victorian period accurately
      and rewardingly, it is necessary to admit and re-
      cover the forms of stylization and convention with
      which Victorian audiences were naturally familiar.
      At present, I hope to indicate how at least one form
      of stylization, which I have called the 'emblem,'
      operates in Victorian literature. In particular, I
      shall examine the emblems of the patient and selfless

woman and the man-destroying woman, which I have
termed the Griselda and the Judith emblems."

        Among examples cited are Thackeray's illustra-
tions to *Vanity Fair*, H. K. Browne's illustrations
to *Dombey and Son* and George H. Thomas' illustrations to *The Last Chronicle of Barset*.

240   Reynolds, Graham. "Charles Dickens and the World of
            Art." *Apollo* ns 91: 422-29.

       Includes mention of his illustrators.

241   Slythe, R. Margaret. *The Art of Illustration 1750-
            1900.* London: The Library Association.

       Brief mention of novel illustration. Various
illustration processes are described.

242   Steig, Michael. "Defining the Grotesque: An
            Attempt at Synthesis." *The Journal of
            Aesthetics and Art Criticism* 29: 253-60.

       An attempt to define the grotesque in art and
literature.

       "The grotesque involves the managing of the
uncanny by the comic. More specifically: a) When
the infantile material is primarily threatening,
comic techniques, including caricature, diminish the
threat through degradation or ridicule; but at the
same time, they may also enhance anxiety through
their aggressive implications and through the
strangeness they lend to the threatening figure. b)
In what is usually called the comic-grotesque, the
comic in its various forms lessens the threat of
identification with infantile drives by means of
ridicule; at the same time, it lulls inhibitions and
makes possible on a preconscious level the same
identification that it appears to the conscience or
superego to prevent. In short, both extreme types
of the grotesque (and there are many instances in
between) return us to childhood--the one attempts a
liberation from fear, while the other attempts a

liberation from inhibition; but in both a state of
unresolved tension is the most common result,
because of the intrapsychic conflicts involved."

243   Steig, Michael. "The Iconography of *David
        Copperfield.*" *Hartford Studies in Literature*
        2: 1-18.

      Despite Dickens' strict control over his illus-
trators, they often contributed details of their own.
H. K. Browne was usually "the originator of allegorical or symbolic details that do not derive from the
text itself."

      Browne's illustrations to *David Copperfield*
"constitute a kind of running commentary on the
text, and they even develop a consistent visual
symbolism of sorts, as in the use of Eve and the
serpent, of masks, angels, and of hidden faces."

244   Steig, Michael. "Iconography of Sexual Conflict in
        Dombey and Son." *Dickens Studies Annual* 1:
        161-67.

      "Despite the story-book romance of Florence and
Walter, the dominant view of relations between the
sexes in *Dombey and Son* is that they involve a
continuing struggle for power in which the female
is the more aggressive antagonist, and most often
the victor. This view is brought out vividly by
certain of the original illustrations which bear
upon the Dombey-Edith-Carker triangle, and by two
others that have to do with Mrs. MacStinger's
campaign to subject Captain Cuttle to permanent
marital thralldom. A study of the evidence of
Dickens' professional relationship with Halbot K.
Browne has led me to conclude that while one may
safely attribute the choice of subject for virtually
all of Phiz's illustrations to Dickens, the minor
details, and in particular those that comment
allegorically (in the form of paintings, posters,
sculpture, and the like) upon the text, can generally
be assumed to be the artist's own contribution. Such
details thus have the status of contemporary critical
commentary of an especially pertinent kind, since
they were created while the novel was in progress

and the illustrator in repeated communication with
the author. At the very least, we can reasonably
assume that such details are consonant with the
author's intention, and at times they serve to
clarify that intention."

245 Steig, Michael. "Structure and the Grotesque in
          Dickens: *Dombey and Son; Bleak House.*" *The
          Centennial Review* 14: 313-30.

          "Nothing more vividly epitomizes the novelty
     of *Bleak House* in Dickens' development than the
     radical innovations of H. K. Browne's etchings.
     Where *Dombey* and *Copperfield* have one 'dark' plate
     apiece, *Bleak House* has ten; and more remarkably,
     of these, six are totally devoid of human figures,
     while in two others such figures are barely dis-
     tinguishable. It is as though the illustrations are
     meant to mirror the emphasis of this novel in which
     external, non-human, or dehumanized entities--fog,
     mud, Chancery, Tom-all-Alone's--have virtually the
     status of characters. For the first time, Dickens
     has truly organized a novel around a comprehensive
     view of the nature of society, a vision of the total
     environment."

246 Szladits, Lola L. *Charles Dickens 1812-1870: An
          Anthology...from Materials in the Berg Col-
          lection of English and American Literature in
          Commemoration of the Centennial of Dickens'
          Death.* New York: New York Public Library and
          Arno Press.

          Original drawings by Dickens' illustrators
     reproduced.

247 Szladits, Lola L. "Dickens and His Illustrators."
          Bulletin of the New York Public Library 74:
          351-53.

          Brief commentary on Dickens' illustrators.

248 Twyman, Michael. *Printing 1770-1970. An Illus-
          trated History of Its Development and Uses in
          England.* London: Eyre & Spottiswoode. See
          Chapter six, "Pictures into print," 85-110.

249 Vogler, Richard Allen. "Cruikshank and Dickens:
          A Review of the Role of Artist and Author."
          Dissertation Abstracts International 34:
          4221A. University of California, Los Angeles.

     "The name Cruikshank precedes Dickens in this
     title because emphasis is placed on the artist
     rather than the writer in discussing works on which
     both men collaborated. With few exceptions previous
     accounts, written by people interested primarily in
     Dickens, have emphasized the unimportance of George
     Cruikshank's role in illustrating *Sketches by Boz,
     Oliver Twist,* and minor works written or edited by
     Dickens. This dissertation places in fairer balance
     the contributions of both men to these works."

     "An appendix consists of a catalogue of
     Cruikshank's known working drawings and tracings
     relating to *Oliver Twist, Sketches by Boz,* and minor
     works associated with both men."

                          1971

250 Borowitz, David. "George Cruikshank: Mirror of an
          Age." *Charles Dickens and George Cruikshank.*
          Papers read at a Clark Library Seminar on May
          9, 1970 by J. Hillis Miller and David Borowitz.
          With an Introduction by Ada B. Nisbet. Los
          Angeles: William Andrews Clark Memorial
          Library, University of California, 71-90.

     "A sampling of the life and work of this great
     genius of the nineteenth century."

251 Cohen, Jane R. "'A Melancholy Clown'--The Relation-
        ship of Robert Seymour and Charles Dickens."
        Harvard Library Bulletin 19: 250-79.

        "Dickens' first illustrator immeasurably aided
     his literary ascent; his second inadvertently sky-
     rocketed him to fame. If the young writer found
     working with established veterans a mixed blessing,
     the consequences for the artists were tragic.
     Cruikshank's extended relationship with Dickens
     contributed to his mental derangement; Robert
     Seymour's brief involvement with the author fatally
     unbalanced a long-disturbed mind. Seymour, who was
     known in the early 1830's for his humorous sporting
     sketches, is remembered now mainly as the first of
     Pickwick's three illustrators; his heirs, like
     Cruikshank, claimed the artist originated a work of
     Dickens. Unlike Cruikshank, Seymour received more
     attention from Dickens after his death than during
     his abbreviated lifetime, but less from posterity
     as an original genius in his own right."

252 Gordon, Catherine. "The Illustration of Sir Walter
        Scott: Nineteenth-Century Enthusiasm and
        Adaptation." *Journal of the Warburg and
        Courtauld Institutes* 34: 297-317.

        Illustrated editions of Scott in the nineteenth
     century.

253 Hemstedt, Geoffrey Colin. "Some Victorian Novels
        and Their Illustrations." *Dissertation
        Abstracts International* 35: 368A-83A.
        Princeton University.

        The chronological study of novel illustration
     reveals a "normalization of style, away from carica-
     ture and the grotesque towards natural representa-
     tion," which could be said "to correspond to a
     comparable change in narrative preoccupation, with
     the exclusion of fantasy and free invention in
     favour of a flatter realism." But with this
     "normalization of style" comes the readers' growing
     dissatisfaction with the obtrusion of a firm image
     of what should properly exist in our own picturing
     imaginations. "The illustration becomes progressively

less controversial, and is finally removed
altogether."

254 Hunt, John Dixon. "Dickens and the Traditions of
         Graphic Satire." *Encounters: Essays on
         Literature and the Visual Arts*. Ed. John
         Dixon Hunt. London: Studio Vista, 124-55.

     "Dickens drew upon and was conditioned by the
same graphic traditions that gave him his
illustrators."

     "It would appear that such early works as the
Sketches and *Pickwick Papers* were directly nourished
by the world of graphic journalism and that the
large readership Dickens soon commanded is perhaps
a measure of his success in extending into literary
form the topics, treatment and attitudes of popular
engravings." "In the later novels Dickens's
imagination is sustained on many occasions that we
admire most in his art by the techniques and ideas
suggested by the graphic arts."

     The traditions of graphic satire taught Dickens
to perceive the inevitable connections "between
fantasy and reality, between 'prevailing idea' and
the multitudinous world of rich detail."

255 McMaster, Juliet. *Thackeray: The Major Novels*.
         Toronto: University of Toronto Press.

     Contains commentary on the illustrations in
Thackeray's novels.

256 Miller, J. Hillis. "The Fiction of Realism:
         Sketches by Boz, Oliver Twist, and Cruikshank's
         Illustrations." *Dickens Centennial Essays*.
         Ed. Ada Nisbet and Blake Nevius. Berkeley, Los
         Angeles, London: University of California
         Press, 85-153. Also in *Charles Dickens and
         George Cruikshank*. Papers read at a Clark
         Library Seminar on May 9, 1970 by J. Hillis
         Miller and David Borowitz. With an Introduction

by Ada B. Nisbet. Los Angeles: William Andrews
Clark Memorial Library, University of California,
1971, 1-69.

"To raise the question of what it means to
have an illustrated book, to set Cruikshank's etchings and Dickens's *Sketches* side by side, or to
investigate either separately...is to encounter a
contradictory vibration between a mimetic reading
sustained by reference to something extra-artistic
and a reading which sees both the literary text and
its illustrations as fictions. The meaning of such
fictions is constituted and maintained only by
their reference to other equally fictional entities.
This reciprocally sustaining, reciprocally destroy-
ing vacillation between literal and figurative
interpretations is crucial to the process of expli-
cating both graphic and literary works."

257   Muir, Percy. *Victorian Illustrated Books.* New
        York: Praeger.

A survey of nineteenth-century English book
illustration with some attention paid to novel
illustration. Commentary on Cruikshank as illustrator for Ainsworth and Dickens, on H. K. Browne
as illustrator for Charles Lever and Dickens and
on Richard Doyle, John Leech, Charles Keene, George
du Maurier and J. E. Millais.

258   Paroissien, David. "*Pictures from Italy* and its
        Original Illustrator." *The Dickensian* 67:
        87-90.

Speculations about the reasons Samuel Palmer
replaced Clarkson Stanfield as the illustrator of
the first edition of Dickens' *Pictures from Italy.*
Stanfield may have withdrawn from the work because
"he felt compromised by the book's marked anti-
Catholicism and unsympathetic view of Italy."

259   Paulson, Ronald. *Hogarth: His Life, Art, and Times.*
        2 vols. Published for the Paul Mellon Centre

for Studies of British Art (London), Ltd. New
Haven: Yale University Press.

Valuable background for any study of nineteenth-
century illustration.

260   Steig, Michael. "*David Copperfield,* Plate I: A
Note on Phiz and Hogarth." *Dickens Studies
Newsletter* 2: 55-56.

Hogarth's engraving, "The Sleeping Congrega-
tion" (1736), is the probable source of Browne's
Plate 1 in *David Copperfield,* "Our Pew at Church."

1972

261   Cardwell, Margaret. Appendices E. and H.: "The
illustrations" and "The proof sent to the
illustrator." *The Mystery of Edwin Drood.* By
Charles Dickens. Oxford: Clarendon Press,
238-42, 256-69.

Commentary on Charles Collins' and Luke Fildes'
illustrations to the novel.

262   Ovenden, Graham, ed. *The Illustrators of "Alice in
Wonderland" and "Through the Looking Glass."*
Introduction by John Davis. New York: St.
Martin's Press; London: Academy Editions.

A survey of the illustrators of Lewis Carroll's
Alice's Adventures in Wonderland and *Through the
Looking Glass and What Alice Found There.*

263   Steig, Michael. "The Critic and the Illustrated
Novel: Mr. Turveydrop from Gillray to *Bleak
House.*" *The Huntington Library Quarterly* 36:
55-67.

Criticism of Victorian illustrated novels has
so far lacked "any developed discussion of the
aesthetics of the Dickens-Browne novel, including
such questions as how the presence of the illustrations makes the reader's experience significantly
different; what are the characteristic modes of
integration of text and pictures; and how the
various sources--which include not only caricature,
but emblem books, mythology, and drama--drawn upon
in these illustrations relate to the problem of
integration."

"Rather than seeing *Bleak House* as having
moved away from the traditions of English caricature, we should perhaps say that the English novel
and its readers were by 1853 quite far from those
traditions, and that *Bleak House* represents a late,
brilliant attempt to incorporate the traditional
techniques so characteristic of Hogarth, Gillray,
the Cruikshanks, Seymour, and others. And perhaps
it is only now, with the historical distance of
another century, that we can begin to experience the
full effect of *Bleak House* as its creators intended."

264   Steig, Michael. "*Martin Chuzzlewit*'s Progress by
          Dickens and Phiz." *Dickens Studies Annual* 2:
          119-49.

"I have argued elsewhere that *Martin Chuzzlewit*
is the first of the Dickens-Browne collaborations
to reflect a shift in the illustrator's manner
toward a relative realism of character portrayal;
but it is also the first of the three Dickens novels
that are most Hogarthian in their illustrations, in
that the plates are most heavily crammed with
emblematic details and contain a large number of
parallels between one plate and another. Along
these lines, *Martin Chuzzlewit* is of particular
interest in having an allegorical wrapper and
frontispiece which are directly related, and in being
the only novel for which survive Dickens' instructions regarding several successive plates containing
emblematic details. Although the *Chuzzlewit* illustrations present no simple, unified sequence depict-
ing something like 'The Hypocrite's Progress,' there
are, among the forty plates, decided affinities with

Hogarth's great 'progresses,' and these illustrations
thus deserve, both individually and collectively,
the closest attention."

265   Vogler, Richard A.   "*Oliver Twist*:   Cruikshank's
          Pictorial Prototypes." *Dickens Studies Annual*
          2:   98-118.

      "In attempting to strengthen the case for
establishing a claim to his role in *Oliver Twist*,
George Cruikshank never mentioned those of his own
published etchings which offer obvious prototypes
for characters in *Oliver Twist* even though he used
far less concrete kinds of evidence to show that he
was the originator of characters and plot elements
in the novel. Apparently it did not occur to the
artist that such forerunners for characters in the
novel (rather than his unpublished preliminary
sketches) offer a strong claim for his possible
influence on the author. The external evidence
contained in these published prototypes has nothing
to do with the Cruikshank-Dickens controversy or
with any claims made by the artist himself, but
rather offers the best kind of supporting evidence
that Cruikshank, before he met Charles Dickens, al-
ready had in his repertoire the stock figures or
pictorial prototypes of characters that were to
reappear in *Oliver Twist*....The existence in
Cruikshank's published etchings of forerunners for
characters in the novel indicates the extent to which
Cruikshank may have suggested, directly or indirect-
ly, characters and even incidents in the plot to the
young Dickens."

                          1973

266   Cardwell, Margaret.   "Dickens's Correspondence with
          the Illustrator of *Edwin Drood*." *The*
          Dickensian 69:   42-43.

      Letters from Dickens to Luke Fildes in the
Gimbel collection in the Beinecke Rare Book and
Manuscript Library at Yale.

267 Richards, B. A. "The Use of the Visual Arts in the
        Nineteenth-century Novel." Oxford, England.
        Dissertation.

268 Steig, Michael. "Cruikshank's Peacock Feathers in
        Oliver Twist." *Ariel* 4: 49-53.

        The peacock feathers included in a Cruikshank
     etching originally designed for the final chapter of
     Oliver Twist may represent "a private comment by the
     artist. As such, they could imply that the happy
     resolution depicted is only temporary, and that mis-
     fortune will dog these characters after the conclu-
     sion of the novel. There is also conceivably a
     hint that Rose's marriage will not last, given the
     association of peacock feathers with spinsterhood;
     and further, there may even be a sardonic comment
     upon the complacency and pride of these comfortably
     middle-class characters."

269 Thomas, Deborah Allen. "MLA Seminar 62, 'Dickens
        and the Graphic Arts.'" *Dickens Studies News-
        letter* 4: 5-7.

        Account of seminar on Dickens' relationship
     with the graphic arts. Participating in the dis-
     cussion were Harry Stone, John Harvey, Anthony
     Burton, Michael Steig and Robert Patten.

270 Tye, J. R. "Legal Caricature: Cruikshank Analogues
        to the *Bleak House* Cover." *The Dickensian* 69:
        39-41.

        Possible influence of a Cruikshank illustration
     to Gilbert à Beckett's *The Comic Blackstone* on
     Dickens or Hablot Browne in designing the cover for
     the monthly parts of *Bleak House*.

271 Wakeman, Geoffrey. *Victorian Book Illustration:
        The Technical Revolution*. Newton Abbot, Devon:
        David & Charles.

272 Wertheim, Albert. "Childhood in John Leech's
          'Pictures of Life and Character.'" *Victorian
          Studies* 17: 75-87.

     Leech's *Punch* cartoons and the view they
provide of Victorian children.

1974

273 Blake, Quentin. "Doing All the Voices--Quentin
          Blake Discusses the Drawings of George
          Cruikshank." *The Listener* 91: 313-14.

     Comment on the Cruikshank exhibition at the
Victoria and Albert Museum.

274 Burton, Anthony. "Cruikshank as an Illustrator of
          Fiction." *George Cruikshank: A Revaluation.*
          Ed. Robert L. Patten. *The Princeton University
          Library Chronicle* 35: 93-128.

     "There is much more in the *Oliver Twist* illus-
trations than the frantic gloom of 'Fagin in the
condemned Cell.' Among Cruikshank's illustrations
to works of fiction, the *Oliver Twist* plates are the
prime example of his ability to make his designs
sustain a narrative. They are not merely visualiza-
tions of disconnected moments in the author's story;
they are themselves connected by various means, so
as to form a sequence. A sequential element is to
be seen also in the illustrations to *Peter Schlemihl,
Robinson Crusoe,* and *Jack Sheppard.* In the last,
Cruikshank experiments with variation of pace in his
visual narrative, and in the *Oliver Twist* plates he
seeks, by repetition, a cumulative effect and an
effect of dramatic irony. In the case of *Jack
Sheppard* and *Oliver Twist,* it was no doubt the
conditions of monthly publication that disposed
Cruikshank towards the creation of visual narratives;
he absorbed the verbal narrative little by little,
never seeing it whole, and so his illustrations reflect his developing understanding of it."

"He has extremely well conveyed the dominant
mood of *Oliver Twist*, the mood of anxious expecta-
tion that is generated by a story of subjection and
liberation, of oppression and compassion, of exclu-
sion and inclusion. It is such themes as these that
have inspired Cruikshank to his most compelling
illustrations for other works."

275 Burton, Anthony. "Thackeray's Collaboration with
         Cruikshank, Doyle, and Walker." *Costerus* n.s.
         2: 141-84.

     A review of Thackeray's collaboration with
George Cruikshank, Richard Doyle and Fred Walker.
Thackeray himself "had a talent for comic draughtsmanship which he put to good use in his own highly
individual type of illustration. And he understood
the work of other Victorian graphic humourists well
enough to enable him to elicit good work from them
when they illustrated his works."

276 Cardwell, Margaret. "A Newly-Discovered Version of
         a Collins Sketch for *Edwin Drood*." *The
         Dickensian* 70: 31-34.

     Account of the discovery of an unpublished
sketch drawn by Charles Collins for *The Mystery of
Edwin Drood*.

     See Lehmann-Haupt, 66.

277 Dickens, Charles. *The Letters of Charles Dickens.
         Volume Three 1842-1843*. Ed. Madeline House,
         Graham Storey and Kathleen Tillotson. The
         Pilgrim Edition. Oxford: Clarendon Press.

278 Feaver, William. "'At it Again': Aspects of
         Cruikshank's Later Work." *George Cruikshank:
         A Revaluation*. Ed. Robert L. Patten. *The
         Princeton University Library Chronicle* 35:
         249-58.

"As things stood in the 1840s Cruikshank's
only resort was his Cause; far from being a disas-
trous turn in his career   Temperance provided him
with a sense of direction and purpose which reani-
mated his art. Naturally the several aspects of his
work remained interlinked. Temperance beliefs
seeped, to Dickens' dismay, into his *Fairy Library*
illustrations..., and the subject matter of much of
his later work, the 1851 Exhibition for instance,
tended to reappear from time to time with fresh
moral underlinings. But the temperance ideas--which
were concerned, after all, with every part of mid-
Victorian society--did serve to concentrate
Cruikshank's mind wonderfully. For the good of the
Cause he looked back to Hogarth's guiding, popular-
izing principles, discarding virtuosity and all
thought of art for art's sake in favor of a more
straight-forward style; suiting his means to the
great end he had in mind."

279   Fowles, John. "Introduction: Remembering
        Cruikshank." *George Cruikshank: A Revaluation.*
        Ed. Robert L. Patten. *The Princeton University
        Library Chronicle* 35: xiii-xvi.

"I detect two great figures behind Cruikshank.
The first is Hogarth, of course. Cruikshank never
mastered oil, and given the age-old European award
of primacy to that medium, I suppose he has to be
placed on a lower pinnacle. But I suspect that if
he and Hogarth had been Japanese, it might well have
been the latter who now stood in the shade. Lists
of artistic merit are strictly for fools, however,
and the important thing is that these two English
graphic masters did share, behind their personal
neuroses, their particular exaggerations, an identity
of spirit. They both attacked hypocrisy and anything that smelt of the complacent Establishment;
more interested in man himself than in nature, they
had the city in their blood; and for all their
ruthless attacks on the stupidity and bestiality of
Homo sapiens, they never lost faith in his essential
humanity."

280 Harvey, John. "George Cruikshank: A Master of the
     Poetic Use of Line." *George Cruikshank: A
     Revaluation*. Ed. Robert L. Patten. *The
     Princeton University Library Chronicle* 35:
     129-55.

     "Though it seems undeniable to me, and always
     worth saying, that an artist cannot be great if the
     developed interests of the eye do not cooperate
     with the deepest interests of the man; without the
     interests of the eye one does not have an artist of
     any kind. And the art of Cruikshank, though he him-
     self is not the greatest kind of artist, expresses
     not only the deep concern of the man, but intense
     visual interests that make him, specifically, the
     most versatile genius in the use of line that
     English art has seen. It is above all his power of
     line that makes him a major etcher and draughtsman
     for wood; it is a power that makes the range of
     things Beardsley can do with his pen seem impover-
     ished, and frigidly deliberate and hard even in his
     complicated sensualities. However, because
     Cruikshank's line changed so much in character and
     quality through his long working life, an attempted
     account of its strength needs to be also a chrono-
     logical account."

281 Horsman, Alan. Appendix E: "The illustrations."
     Dombey and Son. By Charles Dickens. Oxford:
     Clarendon Press, 865-71.

     Commentary on Browne's illustrations.

282 James, Louis. "An Artist in Time: George
     Cruikshank in Three Eras." *George Cruikshank:
     A Revaluation*. Ed. Robert L. Patten. *The
     Princeton University Library Chronicle* 35:
     157-68.

     An analysis of one polemical work from each of
     three "eras" in Cruikshank's work in an "attempt to
     suggest some of the graphic conventions within which
     Cruikshank worked, and which he made his own."

     "Intimately involved with social and even poli-
     tical issues as it was, his art was primarily the

creative work of the poet, a poet as Keats saw
Shakespeare, with the genius of negative capability.
He 'is the most unpoetical of any thing in existence; because he has no Identity--he is continually
in for--and filling some other Body....' This to
some extent explains his claims to works he illustrated, such as *Oliver Twist*: he became what he
drew. But he was also instinctively in touch with
the wider modality and convention of each age in
which he worked, its sensibilities, mental struc-
tures, and iconography. Cruikshank tells us so much
about the nineteenth century because he shows us not
only what it experienced, but also the ways in which
it felt and communicated."

283 Johnson, E. D. H. "The George Cruikshank Collection
        at Princeton." *George Cruikshank: A Revalu-
        ation.* Ed. Robert L. Patten. *The Princeton
        University Library Chronicle* 35: 1-33.

     Outline of Cruikshank's career illustrated by
references to the holdings in the Cruikshank Collection at Princeton.

     "Cruikshank's turn to book illustration in 1823
liberated inherent faculties both for the purely
comic and for the fantastic which lay at the heart
of his vision, but which had hitherto been suppressed
in the service of political satire."

284 Kaufman, Robert Frederick. "The Relationship Be-
        tween Illustration and Text in the Novels of
        Dickens, Thackeray, Trollope and Hardy."
        Dissertation Abstracts International 35:
        4433A-34A. New York University.

     "While illustrations added enjoyment and under-
standing to the novels, it is almost impossible to
develop any general theory of the relationship between illustration and text that would cover every
novelist. As the Victorian novel became more
internalized, illustrations became less able to make
the reader 'see.'"

285 Kunzle, David. "*Mr. Lambkin*: Cruikshank's Strike
for Independence." *George Cruikshank: A
Revaluation*. Ed. Robert L. Patten. *The
Princeton University Library Chronicle* 35:
169-87.

"Throughout his long career, George Cruikshank
lived in the shadow of Hogarth, whose status as
artist-author he envied. This status seemed to
promise an artistic independence and an economic
security that always eluded Cruikshank. His life
and oeuvre were divided by his principal biographer,
Blanchard Jerrold, into two distinct epochs: Before
Temperance (through 1847) and After Temperance (1848
to his death in 1878), the second being judged at
that time and since as incomparably less fertile
than the first. At the junction of these two periods
stands his most Hogarthian work, *The Bottle*..., with
its sequel, *The Drunkard's Children*..., perhaps the
artist's last truly creative performance, and his
only truly successful attempt to combine the coveted
dual role of artist-as-author. *The Bottle* has,
however, a close chronological predecessor which is
the only other example in Cruikshank's immense oeuvre
of independent pictorial narrative. This work, which
is called *Mr. Lambkin*...for short, has been little
regarded, probably because it is graphically not
very striking, nor does it share the particular biographical or controversial interest of the book-
illustrations which preceded it. The importance of
Cruikshank's first experiment in independent narrative lies principally in the light it sheds on
problems transcending those of the artist's personal
career in particular and touching upon the art of
caricature in general as it adapted to new conditions
and evolved new alternatives."

286 Marten, Harry P. "The Visual Imaginations of
Dickens and Hogarth: Structure and Sense."
Studies in the Novel 6: 145-64.

"The exploration of the congruences of Dickens's
world and Hogarth's in matters of overall structural
construction and depiction of scene makes Dickens's
fiction more comprehensible, providing a meaningful
point of departure for a reevaluation of what is old
and new in a writer who continues to please in count-
less ways."

287 Matthews, Maleen. "Illustrators of *A Christmas Carol.*" *Country Life* 156: 1730-32.

288 Melville, Robert. "Fagin and Co." *New Statesman* 87: 557-58.

     Review of Cruikshank exhibition at the Victoria and Albert Museum.

289 Neve, Christopher. "Cruikshank's Comet." *Country Life* 155: 776.

     Brief appreciation.

290 Page, Norman. "Thomas Hardy's Forgotten Illustrators." *Bulletin of the New York Public Library* 77: 456-64.

     "Hardy's fiction, as might be expected of one who was both a poet and a draughtsman, is often sharply visual in conception; it might therefore have offered an artist an unusually attractive prospect. But as he wrote for a wide variety of magazines and was subject (as Dickens was not) to the authority of editors, Hardy never achieved the close integration of illustrations with his text. Dickens, with his dynamic and assertive nature, insisted on getting from his artists what he wanted. In his quieter way Hardy succeeded in exercising a good deal of influence over their work..., and there can be little doubt that these long-neglected illustrations embody some of the novelist's own ideas and intentions. Although some of his illustrators on their intrinsic merits deserve no more than a continuance of their obscurity, others--notably Hatherell--have suffered an injustice at the hands of publishers and editors; and there is surely a case to be made for restoring the best of their work in future editions of the novels. Without it, we can certainly not expect to be able to recreate the experience of Hardy's original readers."

291 Paulson, Ronald. "The Tradition of Comic Illustra-
          tion from Hogarth to Cruikshank." *George
          Cruikshank: A Revaluation.* Ed. Robert L.
          Patten. *The Princeton University Library
          Chronicle* 35: 35-60.

     "Dickens, like Hogarth, was consciously desert-
ing the texts of contemporary novelists and their
conventions, turning back to the streets of London,
its popular theater, and its popular prints (with
a long look back at Hogarth). His particular sort
of amalgam of literary and graphic conventions with
conventions with contemporary sign systems occurs
when a writer or artist consciously reacts against
old texts and *topoi.* Dickens himself represents
the verbal equivalent of the beginning of the comic
tradition in Hogarth's *Hudibras* and *A Harlot's
Progress,* while Cruikshank represents the end of it,
the artist returning from emblem to illustration
and putting himself back in the hands of his author."

292 Shillingsburg, Peter L. "Thackeray Texts: A Guide
          to Inexpensive Editions." *Costerus* ns 2:
          287-313.

     "A kind of consumer's report" examining the
text and critical apparatus of each practical edition of Thackeray's works currently in print.
"There is not one Thackeray text anywhere that mea-
sures up to the demands of modern scholarship or
which approaches the standards of the Clarendon
editions of Dickens and the Brontës, much less those
of the Wesleyan Fielding edition. And as for
practical editions, with the exception of *Vanity
Fair,* Thackeray texts are a disaster."

293 Sorenson, Gerald C. "Thackeray Texts and Biblio-
          graphical Scholarship." *Costerus* ns 2: 267-
          85.

     "Thackeray texts present in very clear form the
variety of problems that confront the editor of
nineteenth-century English fiction." "The illustrations in a Thackeray novel, whether dropped into the
text or not, are anything but incidental; the editor
cannot afford to ignore them. They must in fact be

treated as we have been accustomed to treat sub-
stantive textual readings."

294   Steig, Michael. "George Cruikshank and the Gro-
        tesque: A Psychodynamic Approach." *George
        Cruikshank: A Revaluation.* Ed. Robert L.
        Patten. *The Princeton University Library
        Chronicle* 35: 189-211.

"In his grotesque work Cruikshank draws upon
fantasies of one's own and others' aggression, of
chaos, engulfment, being devoured, and of childhood
sexual confusion and desire, and in particular
childhood ideas about the body. There is no direct
correlation of political views with these uses of
fantasy material, although Cruikshank's later state-
ments about his youthful radicalism and growing
conservatism, though of questionable accuracy, are
probably not irrelevant to his development as an
artist. In various ways, he employs comedy,
ridicule, symmetry and line to manage (or, in psycho-
analytic terms, defend against) the various anx-
ieties aroused."

"If there is any validity in the notion that
our deepest responses to art are governed by the way
art simultaneously arouses and manages or defends
against anxiety, then surely the grotesque, with its
mixtures of fear and comedy, the beautiful and the
ugly, should be an artistic realm usefully ap-
proached through an analysis based on such an assump-
tion. An artist like George Cruikshank, whose
methods and subjects are so various, will perhaps
always ultimately elude attempts to fix him criti-
cally under any rubric. But given the difficulty of
even talking about such a complex creative genius,
we must find or invent languages which facilitate
such discussion. And I trust that the particular
variety of critical language I have developed here
will, despite its limitations, have illuminated an
important facet of Cruikshank's work, and helped
to make further, more intensive studies possible."

295   Stevens, Joan. "Thackeray's Pictorial Capitals."
        Costerus ns 2: 113-40.

Thackeray's woodcuts drawn to decorate the
initial capitals of his chapters in the original
publications of *Vanity Fair, Pendennis, The
Virginians, Lovel the Widower* and *The Adventures of
Philip* comment on his narrative and help define his
authorial attitude. The vignette capitals fore-
shadow events, offer "generalized comment on the
action," embody "by means of a traditional reference
the basic moral implications of what lies ahead"
or simply add a "visual dimension to forthcoming
words."

296 Stevens, Joan. *"Vanity Fair* and the London Sky-
         line." *Costerus* ns 2: 13-41.

Thackeray's design for the cover of the original parts-issue of *Vanity Fair* indicates a setting
within Hyde Park near Apsley House and is "one of
the clues, not only to the setting and the central
event of the novel, but to its narrative tone and
its pointed relevance to 'English Society' at the
time."

297 Stone, Harry. "Dickens, Cruikshank, and Fairy
         Tales." *George Cruikshank: A Revaluation.*
         Ed. Robert L. Patten. *The Princeton University
         Library Chronicle* 35: 213-247.

"More and more through the 1840s and the early
1850s Dickens was coming to regard the fairy tale
as a paradigm of imaginative art. The fairy tale
was an emblem, at once rudimentary and pure, of
what contemporary society needed and what it increas-
ingly lacked. The fairy tale was also inextricably
associated with childhood; it shaped the very character of future generations. In Dickens' lexicon the
fairy tale was becoming a shorthand way of emphasiz-
ing a contemporary danger and suggesting an essential
solution. The lesson, Dickens felt, was clear. In
an age when men were becoming machines, art--and that
quintessential childhood version of art, the fairy
tale--must be cherished and must be allowed to do
its beneficent work of nurturing man's birthright of
feeling and fancy."

Cruikshank's *Hop-o'-my-Thumb* suggested to Dickens "that Cruikshank was tampering with the sources of imagination and creativity."

"From Dickens' point of view, Cruikshank's didacticism was doubly subversive. It intruded a prosing note that was totally alien to the spirit and tone of the fairy tale. But more important, it imported into the world of the fairy tale the anti-fairy tale. Enticed by Cruikshank's compelling illustrations, the child would enter the fairy-tale world only to find that it contained the same prosing precepts that nagged at him from the pages of his insufferable copybooks or his improving moral tracts. To Dickens, Cruikshank's text was a fraud. It would turn children away from the fount of fancy and imagination at the very source."

298 Sweeney, Patricia Runk. "Thackeray's Best Illustrator." *Costerus* ns 2: 83-111.

Thackeray's illustrations serve three purposes: "some simply complement text (e.g., a portrait of a character whom we wish to visualize), some tell the story pictorially (e.g., a record of an action), and some add a story, or another narrative dimension, to the events being described (e.g., an emblematic capital). They become, then, pictorial literature, and as an aid to the understanding of the mind and the creativity of a great writer, they deserve attention and preservation." Other illustrators of Thackeray's work have not been successful.

299 Vogler, Richard A. "Cruikshank and Dickens: A Reassessment of the Role of the Artist and the Author." *George Cruikshank: A Revaluation.* Ed. Robert L. Patten. *The Princeton University Library Chronicle* 35: 61-91.

"According to Albert M. Cohn, Cruikshank's definitive cataloguer, the artist did illustrations for 863 books and produced over 700 caricatures. Of the 863 books, Dickens wrote only two and edited only two. Obviously the 'central concern' of any competent historian of Cruikshank's seventy-five-year working career could hardly be his brief working

association with Dickens, any more than the central
concern of a Dickens biographer would be that association. The genius of both men is so great that
neither stands to gain or lose from what has been
blown up by Dickensians into the 'Dickens-Cruikshank
controversy,' a dispute which can never be settled
definitively unless new documents, especially the
presumably destroyed letters from Cruikshank to
Dickens, come to light, and probably not even then.
Certainly, the more I examine the immense corpus of
Cruikshank's graphic works the more I have come to
realize the insignificance of what should more
properly be called the 'Forster-Cruikshank controversy' (since Dickens himself wrote not a single
word about it). The Dickens authorities who have
so readily accepted Forster's version have never
taken the trouble to study the visual evidence
supporting Cruikshank's claims, preferring to have
their laugh at an embellished anecdote and to leave
George Cruikshank, the colossus of graphic art of
the last century, climbing lampposts and wallowing
in gutters for almost a century."

1975

300 Bond, W. H. "Wrappers for *The Virginians*: Variants
         Produced by Duplicate Settings." *The Book
         Collector* 24: 553-57.

     Variants in the wrapper for Thackeray's *The
Virginians*.

301 Cardwell, Margaret. "Collins's Sketches for *Edwin
         Drood*: A Postscript." *The Dickensian* 71:
         45-46.

     Description of the Collins sketches described
by Lehmann-Haupt (66) and now in the possession of
Captain Peter Dickens.

     See Cardwell (276) and Lehmann-Haupt (66).

302 Lougy, Robert E. "Vision and Satire: The Warped Looking Glass in *Vanity Fair*." *PMLA* 90: 256-69. See Peter Shillingsburg's criticism and Lougy's reply, *PMLA* 90: 924-25.

Examination of the title-page illustration increases our understanding of the novel.

303 Patten, Robert L. "*Pickwick Papers* and the Development of Serial Fiction." *Rice University Studies* 61: 51-74.

"Accidentally in *Pickwick* Dickens and Chapman and Hall hit upon an arrangement for issuing original works of fiction in serial parts that revolutionized nineteenth-century publishing, distribution, book-selling, author-publisher relations, copyright provisions, and of course fiction itself....The thirty-two page, two-illustration part became a standard to which the public rapidly became accustomed."

304 Shillingsburg, Peter L. "Thackeray's *Pendennis*: A Rejected Page of Manuscript." *Huntington Library Quarterly* 38: 189-95.

"A single sheet...of an early draft preserved at the Huntington Library sheds light on Thackeray's working habits and on the importance of his illustrations."

305 Spencer, Isobel. *Walter Crane*. London: Studio Vista.

Some treatment of his work as novel illustrator.

306 Steig, Michael. "A Chapter of Noses: George Cruikshank's Psychonography of the Nose." *Criticism* 17: 308-25.

"Cruikshank's illustrations for *Oliver Twist*...
represent a mutual artistic fertilization of two
great artists who shared a social insecurity,
ambivalent relations to the father, conflict between
rebellious and ultra-moralistic tendencies, a need
to domineer, as well as a strong capacity for visual
hallucination of the comic and horrible which was
channelled into the artistic production of grotesque
images. A broad view of Cruikshank's artistic work
from youth to old age reveals a series of swings
between the imaginatively untrammelled (though always technically controlled) and the subdued and
idealistic, between rebelliousness and respect-
ability; and even a comparison of some of his
initial drawings with their final form of etchings
reveals poles of spontaneity and control (much more
notable than a similar comparison of the drawings
and etchings of 'Phiz'). Cruikshank's varying
image of himself seems to have a good deal to do
with the complexities of his work, and most important, perhaps, are the ways in which the manifold
elements of his character gave rise to the expression
of insights inexpressible by other means, particularly after the third decade of the nineteenth century.
'Psychonography' may be a base coinage which will be
quickly driven out of circulation, but I find it a
useful way to designate an artist's repeated employ-
ment of a single element--in this case, the nose--to
delineate a range of largely unconscious meaning."

                           1976

307   Cohen, Jane R.   "The Portrayal of Sir John Chester
         by Browne and Cattermole." *The Dickensian* 72:
         93-97.

      The importance of various individual illustra-
tions in Dickens' novels "usually has been stressed
at the expense of their function as part of a
sequence."

      The importance of the sequential element in the
plates is compellingly demonstrated "by the graphic
portrayal of John Chester throughout *Barnaby Rudge*"
by both Hablot Browne and by George Cattermole.

308 Gardner, Joseph H. "Pecksniff's Profession: Boz,
        Phiz, and Pugin." *The Dickensian* 72: 75-86.

     In his illustrations for Dickens' *Martin
Chuzzlewit*, Hablot Browne used emblematic details
based on A. W. N. Pugin's *Contrasts*, first published
in 1836.

309 Gneiting, Teona Tone. "The Pencil's Role in *Vanity
        Fair*." *The Huntington Library Quarterly* 39:
        171-202.

     "Thackeray's illustrations operate...like so
many small windows to let in the fresh air of
reality upon the sometimes stifling atmosphere of
the novel tradition he was debunking and the society
of which he was a part."

310 Guiliano, Edward, introd. "Lewis Carroll as Artist:
        Fifteen Sketches for the *Sylvie and Bruno*
        Books." *Lewis Carroll Observed: A Collection
        of Unpublished Photographs, Drawings, Poetry,
        and New Essays*. Ed. Edward Guiliano. New York:
        Clarkson N. Potter, 145-60.

     Sketches Carroll drew for his *Sylvie and Bruno*
books. Discussion of Carroll's collaboration with
Harry Furniss on the published volumes.

311 Harden, Edgar F. "The Artistry of a Serial Novelist:
        Parts 10, 14, and 15 of *The Newcomes*."
        Studies in English Literature, 1500-1900 16:
        613-30.

     Mention of Thackeray's collaboration with
Richard Doyle.

312 Harden, Edgar F. "The Growth of a Serial Novel:
        Five Installments of *The Newcomes*." *The
        Huntington Library Quarterly* 39: 203-18.

An examination of "the variety and significance
of Thackeray's responses to the challenge of writ-
ing fiction, a challenge intensified in *The Newcomes*
by the purpose of publishing his novel in roughly
equal installments with accompanying illustrations."

313 Life, Allan R. "The Periodical Illustrations of
        John Everett Millais and Their Literary Inter-
        pretation." *Victorian Periodicals Newsletter*
        9: 50-68.

"Admittedly, not all Millais' illustrations
possess the interpretative complexity of his designs
for 'Last Words', 'The Grandmother's Apology', and
'The Bishop and the Knight'. But there are enough
works of this importance among his contributions
to *Once a Week, The Cornhill Magazine,* and other
periodicals to discredit the generalizations that
have discouraged critical investigation of these
designs. Far from being isolated works of art,
insusceptible to literary analysis, the best of
Millais' illustrations are truly interpretative,
embodying through predominantly formal methods
perceptive readings of entire poems. If these works
exemplify a new mode of illustration, it is equal in
literary acumen to the old. If they are naturalis-
tic, they demonstrate that the composition and
rendering of designs can generate thematic content
as readily as conventional iconography, and that
subtly modulated naturalism can be a powerful force
in illustration."

314 Marten, Harry. "Exaggerated Character: A Study of
        the Works of Dickens and Hogarth." *The
        Centennial Review* 20: 290-308.

"Among the enlightening areas of Dickens
criticism still largely unexplored is that of his
artistic relationship" to Hogarth.

"In the area of character delineation particularly, an exploration of what Hogarth's work can tell
us about the novels of the writer who so much valued
it is particularly fruitful."

315   Matthews, Maleen. "Illustrators of Dickens's
          'Chimes.'" *Country Life* 160: 1626-27.

316   Pantazzi, Sybille. "Author and Illustrator: Images
          in Confrontation." *Victorian Periodicals
          Newsletter* 9: 39-49.

          An examination of the common rivalry between
      writer and artist in nineteenth-century periodicals
      and "the uneasy marriage of text and picture which
      resulted from it."

317   Rackin, Donald. "Laughing and Grief: What's So
          Funny About *Alice in Wonderland*?" *Lewis
          Carroll Observed: A Collection of Unpublished
          Photographs, Drawings, Poetry, and New Essays.*
          Ed. Edward Guiliano. New York: Clarkson N.
          Potter, 1-18.

          Comparison of Carroll's original illustrations
      for *Alice's Adventures Under Ground* with Tenniel's
      illustrations suggests that Carroll's illustrations
      "offer a far better companion for both the original
      and the published text."

          "They do so mainly because they better reflect
      the Wonderland horror-comedy that I have been out-
      lining, a horror-comedy that genuinely resides in
      those texts. Thus Tenniel's illustrations, good as
      they are, might well be considered a kind of sugar-
      ing over of the threatening implications of the
      text, the way many daytime reconstructions of night-
      mares sugar over the nightmares' worst episodes.
      Like the shift in titles from 'Under Ground' to the
      rather innocuous 'Wonderland,' this shift from
      Carroll's often horrifying illustrations to Tenniel's
      more comfortable ones fails, of course, to dispel
      the permanent horrors that reside in the very depths
      of Carroll's comic fantasy."

318   Ray, Gordon N. *The Illustrator and the Book in*
         England from 1790 to 1914. New York: Pierpont
         Morgan Library, Oxford University Press.

         "This book began as a catalogue for an exhibi-
      tion at The Pierpont Morgan Library in March and
      April of 1976, but it has ended by being a good deal
      more comprehensive than that exhibition. There
      being no earlier study devoted to a full considera-
      tion of English book illustration between 1790 and
      1914, it seemed unenterprising to limit the works
      described and commented upon to those for the dis-
      play of which space was available. Instead an
      attempt has been made to set forth the subject in
      the sort of detail that would allow its ramifica-
      tions and relationships to be explored with thorough-
      ness and permit major illustrators to be presented
      in depth without slighting lesser figures."

         Reproductions of works by and commentary on
      Cruikshank, Thackeray, Browne, Leech, Doyle, Millais,
      Tenniel, Keene, Du Maurier and others. Includes
      an appendix listing "100 Outstanding Illustrated
      Books Published in England between 1790 and 1914"
      and a useful bibliography.

319   Steig, Michael. "Cruikshank's Nancy." *The*
         Dickensian 72:   87-92.

         "Although Dickens's Nancy is in retrospect a
      single, unified character, in the course of the
      novel she is revealed only gradually, and Cruikshank's
      four Nancies in some ways reflect this development."

APPENDIX A
VICTORIAN ILLUSTRATED NOVELS

AINSWORTH, W. HARRISON.

Rookwood. 1834 (without illustrations). 1836,
George Cruikshank.

Crichton. 1837. Monthly installments in
Ainsworth's Magazine, 1848. H. K. Browne.

Jack Sheppard. Monthly installments in
Bentley's Miscellany, 1839 to 1840.
George Cruikshank.

The Tower of London. Monthly parts, January
1840 to December 1840. George Cruikshank.

Guy Fawkes. Monthly installments in *Bentley's
Miscellany,* January 1840 to November 1841.
George Cruikshank.

Old Saint Paul's. Monthly parts, 1841. John
Franklin.

The Miser's Daughter. Monthly installments in
Ainsworth's Magazine, 1842. George
Cruikshank.

Windsor Castle. Monthly installments in
    Ainsworth's Magazine, 1842 to 1843.
    George Cruikshank, Tony Johannot, W. A.
    Delamotte.

Saint James's. Monthly installments in
    Ainsworth's Magazine, 1844. George
    Cruikshank.

Revelations of London. Monthly installments in
    Ainsworth's Magazine, 1844. H. K. Browne.
    As *Auriol; or, The Elixir of Life*.
    Monthly installments in *The New Monthly
    Magazine*, July 1845 to January 1846.
    H. K. Browne.

James the Second. Monthly installments in
    Ainsworth's Magazine, 1847. R. W. Buss.

Mervyn Clitheroe. Monthly parts, December 1851
    to March 1852 and December 1857 to June
    1858. H. K. Browne.

COCKTON, HENRY.

*The Life and Adventures of Valentine Vox, the
    Ventriloquist*. Monthly parts, 1839 to
    1840. Thomas Onwhyn.

DICKENS, CHARLES.

The Posthumous Papers of the Pickwick Club.
    Monthly parts, April 1836 to November
    1837. Robert Seymour, R. W. Buss,
    H. K. Browne.

Oliver Twist. Monthly installments in *Bentley's
    Miscellany*, February 1837 to April 1839.
    George Cruikshank.

The Life and Adventures of Nicholas Nickleby.
    Monthly parts, April 1838 to October 1839.
    H. K. Browne.

*The Old Curiosity Shop, Master Humphrey's
    Clock*. Weekly parts and monthly numbers,
    25 April 1840 to 6 February 1841. George
    Cattermole, H. K. Browne, Daniel Maclise,
    Samuel Williams.

Barnaby Rudge, Master Humphrey's Clock. Weekly
    parts and monthly numbers, 13 February
    1841 to 27 November 1841. George
    Cattermole, H. K. Browne.

The Life and Adventures of Martin Chuzzlewit.
    Monthly parts, January 1843 to July 1844.
    H. K. Browne.

Dealings with the Firm of Dombey and Son.
    Monthly parts, October 1846 to April 1848.
    H. K. Browne.

*The Personal History, Adventures, Experiences
    and Observations of David Copperfield the
    Younger*. Monthly parts, May 1849 to
    November 1850. H. K. Browne.

Bleak House. Monthly parts, March 1852 to
    September 1853. H. K. Browne.

Little Dorrit. Monthly parts, December 1855
    to June 1857. H. K. Browne.

A Tale of Two Cities. Simultaneously in *All the Year Round,* 30 April to 26 November 1859, and in monthly parts, June 1859 to December 1859. H. K. Browne.

Great Expectations. Weekly installments without illustrations in *All the Year Round,* 1 December 1860 to 3 August 1861. Published in 1862 with illustrations by Marcus Stone.

Our Mutual Friend. Monthly parts, May 1864 to November 1865. Marcus Stone.

The Mystery of Edwin Drood. Monthly parts, April 1870 to September 1870. Luke Fildes.

Christmas Books:

A Christmas Carol. 1843. John Leech.

The Chimes. 1845 (for 1844). Daniel Maclise, John Leech, Richard Doyle, Clarkson Stanfield.

The Cricket on the Hearth. 1846 (for 1845). Daniel Maclise, John Leech, Richard Doyle, Clarkson Stanfield, Edwin Landseer.

The Battle of Life. 1846. Daniel Maclise, John Leech, Richard Doyle, Clarkson Stanfield.

The Haunted Man. 1848. John Leech, Clarkson Stanfield, John Tenniel, F. Stone.

EGAN, PIERCE.

Life in London. Monthly parts, 1820 to 1821. Robert and George Cruikshank.

GASKELL, ELIZABETH.

The Moorland Cottage. 1850. Birket Foster.

Sylvia's Lovers. 1863. George du Maurier.

Wives and Daughters. 1866. George du Maurier.

HARDY, THOMAS.

Far from the Madding Crowd. Monthly installments in *Cornhill Magazine,* January 1874 to December 1874. Helen Paterson Allingham.

The Hand of Ethelberta. Monthly installments in *Cornhill Magazine,* July 1875 to May 1876. George du Maurier.

The Return of the Native. Monthly installments in *Belgravia,* January 1878 to December 1878. Arthur Hopkin.

The Trumpet-Major. Monthly installments in *Good Words,* January 1880 to December 1880. John Collier.

A Laodicean. Monthly installments in *Harper's New Monthly Magazine*, European Edition, December 1880 to December 1881. George du Maurier.

The Mayor of Casterbridge. Weekly installments in *The Graphic*, 2 January 1886 to 15 May 1886. Robert Barnes.

Tess of the D'Urbervilles. Weekly installments in *The Graphic*, 4 July 1891 to 26 December 1891. Hubert von Herkomer and others.

Jude the Obscure. Monthly installments in *Harper's New Monthly Magazine,* December 1894 to November 1895. W. Hatherell.

JAMES, G. P. R.

The Commissioner: or, De Lunatico Inquirendo. Monthly parts, 1841 to 1843. H. K. Browne.

JAMES, HENRY.

Washington Square. Monthly installments in *Cornhill Magazine.* June 1880 to November 1880. George du Maurier.

LEVER, CHARLES.

The Confessions of Harry Lorrequer. Monthly installments in *Dublin University Magazine,* February 1837 to February 1840. Monthly parts, March 1839 to January 1840. H. K. Browne.

Charles O'Malley. Monthly installments in
Dublin University Magazine, March 1840
to 1841. Monthly parts, March 1840 to
December 1841. H. K. Browne.

Jack Hinton, the Guardsman (in *Our Mess*).
Monthly installments in *Dublin University
Magazine,* March 1842 to December 1842.
Monthly parts, January 1842 to December
1842. H. K. Browne.

Tom Burke of 'Ours' (in *Our Mess*). Monthly
parts, February 1843 to September 1844.
H. K. Browne.

Arthur O'Leary. Monthly installments in
Dublin University Magazine, January 1843
to December 1843. 1844, George
Cruikshank.

Tales of the Trains. Monthly installments in
Dublin University Magazine, January 1845
to May 1845. Monthly parts, 1845.
H. K. Browne.

*The O'Donogue: A Tale of Ireland Fifty Years
Ago.* Monthly parts, January 1845 to
November 1845. H. K. Browne.

The Knight of Gwynne. Monthly parts, January
1846 to July 1847. H. K. Browne.

Roland Cashel. Monthly parts, May 1848 to
November 1849. H. K. Browne.

Confessions of Con Cregan, the Irish Gil Blas.
Monthly parts, 1849 to 1850. H. K. Browne.

The Daltons, or Three Roads in Life. Monthly
parts, April 1851 to April 1852. H. K.
Browne.

The Dodd Family Abroad. Monthly parts, September 1852 to April 1854. H. K. Browne.

The Martins of Cro' Martin. Monthly parts, December 1854 to June 1856. H. K. Browne.

Davenport Dunn: A Man of Our Day. Monthly parts, July 1857 to April 1859. H. K. Browne.

One of Them. Monthly parts, December 1859 to January 1861. H. K. Browne.

Barrington. Monthly parts, February 1862 to January 1863. H. K. Browne.

Luttrell of Arran. Monthly parts, December 1863 to February 1865. H. K. Browne.

MAYHEW, AUGUSTUS.

Paved with Gold, or the Romance and Reality of the London Streets. Monthly parts, 1857 to 1858. Richard Doyle, John Leech.

MAYHEW, AUGUSTUS AND HENRY.

The Greatest Plague of Life. Monthly parts, 1847. George Cruikshank.

Whom to Marry and How to Get Married! Monthly parts, 1847 to 1848. George Cruikshank.

The Image of His Father. Monthly parts, 1848. H. K. Browne.

MEREDITH, GEORGE.

    Evan Harrington. Weekly installments in *Once a Week,* 11 February 1860 to 13 October 1860. Charles Keene.

    The Adventure of Harry Richmond. Monthly installments in *Cornhill Magazine,* September 1870 to November 1871. George du Maurier.

REYNOLDS, G. W. M.

    Robert Macaire in England. 1840. H. K. Browne.

SURTEES, ROBERT SMITH.

    Jorricks's Jaunts and Jollities. Monthly installments in *The New Sporting Magazine,* July 1831 to September 1834. 1838, H. K. Browne.

    Soapey Sponge's Sporting Tour. Monthly installments in *The New Monthly Magazine,* January 1849 to December 1851. Monthly parts, 1852 to 1853. John Leech.

    'Ask Mamma.' Monthly parts, 1857 to 1858. John Leech.

    'Plain or Ringlets?' Monthly parts, 1859 to 1860. John Leech.

    Mr Facey Romford's Hounds. Monthly parts, 1864 to 1865. John Leech, H. K. Browne.

THACKERAY, WILLIAM MAKEPEACE.

Vanity Fair. Monthly parts, January 1847 to
    July 1848. W. M. Thackeray.

The History of Pendennis. Monthly parts,
    November 1848 to December 1850. W. M.
    Thackeray.

The Newcomes. Monthly parts, October 1853 to
    August 1855. Richard Doyle.

The Virginians. Monthly parts, November 1857
    to September 1859. W. M. Thackeray.

Lovel the Widower. Monthly installments in
    Cornhill Magazine, January 1860 to June
    1860. W. M. Thackeray.

The Adventures of Philip. Monthly installments
    in *Cornhill Magazine*, January 1861 to
    August 1862. Frederick Walker, W. M.
    Thackeray.

Denis Duval. Monthly installments in *Cornhill
    Magazine*, March 1864 to June 1864.
    Frederick Walker, W. M. Thackeray.

TROLLOPE, ANTHONY.

Framley Parsonage. Monthly installments in
    Cornhill Magazine, January 1860 to April
    1861. J. E. Millais.

Orley Farm. Monthly parts, March 1861 to
    October 1862. J. E. Millais.

The Small House at Allington. Monthly
installments in *Cornhill Magazine,*
September 1862 to April 1864. J. E.
Millais.

Can You Forgive Her? Monthly parts, January
1864 to August 1865. H. K. Browne, "Miss
Taylor."

The Last Chronicle of Barset. Weekly parts,
1 December 1866 to 6 July 1867. George
H. Thomas.

The Claverings. Monthly installments in
Cornhill Magazine, February 1866 to May
1869. M. Ellen Edwards.

Phineas Finn. Monthly installments in *St.
Paul's Magazine,* October 1867 to May 1869.
J. E. Millais.

He Knew He Was Right. Weekly parts, 17
October 1868 to 22 May 1869. Marcus
Stone.

The Vicar of Bullhampton. Monthly parts, July
1869 to May 1870. H. Woods.

Ralph the Heir. Monthly parts, January 1870
to July 1871. F. A. Fraser.

The Golden Lion of Granpère. Monthly installments in *Good Words,* January 1872 to
August 1872. F. A. Fraser.

Phineas Redux. Weekly installments in *The
Graphic,* 19 July 1873 to 10 January 1874.
Frank Holl.

The Way We Live Now. Monthly parts, February
     1874 to September 1875. Luke Fildes?

Marion Fay. Weekly installments in *The
     Graphic,* 3 December 1881 to 3 June 1882.
     W. Small.

Kept in the Dark. Monthly installments in
     Good Words, May 1882 to December 1882.
     One illustration by J. E. Millais.

TROLLOPE, FRANCES.

*The Life and Adventures of Jonathan Jefferson
     Whitlaw.* 1836. Auguste Hervieu.

The Vicar of Wrexhill. 1837. Auguste
     Hervieu.

The Life and Adventures of Michael Armstrong.
     Monthly parts, March 1839 to February
     1840. Auguste Hervieu, Thomas Onwhyn,
     R. W. Buss.

The Widow Married. Monthly installments in
     The New Monthly Magazine, May 1839 to
     June 1840. R. W. Buss.

Charles Chesterfield. Monthly installments in
     The New Monthly Magazine, July 1840 to
     November 1841. H. K. Browne.

The Barnabys in America. Monthly installments
     in *The New Monthly Magazine,* April 1842
     to September 1843. John Leech.

APPENDIX B
VICTORIAN NOVEL ILLUSTRATORS

BROWNE, HABLOT KNIGHT (1815-1882)

    Pseudonym "Phiz." Attended a "life" school in
St. Martin's Lane where William Etty was a
fellow-student. In 1836 first associated with
Dickens. Illustrated *The Pickwick Papers*
(1836-37), *Nicholas Nickleby* (1838-39), *The
Old Curiosity Shop* (1840-41), *Barnaby Rudge*
(1841), *Martin Chuzzlewit* (1843-44), *Dombey
and Son* (1846-48), *David Copperfield* (1849-50),
Bleak House (1852-53), *Little Dorrit* (1855-57)
and *A Tale of Two Cities* (1859). For Charles
Lever he illustrated many novels. Exhibited
water-color drawings at British Institution and
Society of British Artists exhibitions.

BUSS, R. W. (1804-1875)

    Painted theatrical portraits, historical and
humorous genre painting. Illustrated Chaucer,
Shakespeare, edited the *Fine Art Almanack*.
Attempted illustrations for *The Pickwick Papers*
after the death of Seymour.

CATTERMOLE, GEORGE (1800-1868)

    Began exhibiting at the Royal Academy in 1819.
In 1833 became a member of the Society of
Painters in Water Colour. His best-known book
illustrations were for Dickens' *Master Humphrey's
Clock* (1840-41).

CRUIKSHANK, GEORGE (1792-1878)

> Son of the caricaturist and water-color painter
> Isaac Cruikshank and younger brother of the
> caricaturist and miniature painter Robert. No
> formal art training. Produced social and
> political caricatures in the Gillray manner
> and many book illustrations. In 1837 began
> his association with *Bentley's Miscellany*
> where his illustrations to Dickens' *Oliver
> Twist* (1837-39) and W. H. Ainsworth's *Jack
> Sheppard* (1839-40) first appeared. For
> Ainsworth he contributed much of his best work
> as book illustrator. His teetotalist designs
> for *The Bottle* (1847) and *The Drunkard's
> Children* (1848) show his debt to Hogarth. In
> later years he turned to oil painting.

DOYLE, RICHARD (1824-1883)

> Son of the painter and caricaturist John Doyle
> (H.B.). Taught drawing by his father. In
> 1843 became a regular contributor to *Punch* for
> which he drew "Manners and Customs of ye
> Englyshe." In 1850 resigned from *Punch*
> because of that paper's stand on the "papal
> aggression." After this time devoted his tal-
> ents to book illustration and water-color draw-
> ing. Among his finest illustrated books:
> W. M. Thackeray, *Rebecca and Rowena* (1850),
> John Ruskin, *King of the Golden River* (1851)
> and W. M. Thackeray, *The Newcomes* (1853-55).

DU MAURIER, GEORGE (1834-1896)

> Born and educated in Paris. Studied chemistry
> at University College, London; studied art in
> Paris and in Antwerp. Joined regular staff of
> *Punch* in 1864 as successor to John Leech.
> Among his finest illustrated novels are
> Elizabeth Gaskell's *Sylvia's Lovers* (1863) and
> *Wives and Daughters* (1866). Illustrated his

own novels *Peter Ibbetson* (1891), *Trilby*
(1894) and *The Martian* (1896).

FILDES, SIR LUKE (1844-1927)

Best known as a portrait painter. Illustrated
Dickens' *The Mystery of Edwin Drood* and
Trollope's *The Way We Live Now*[?]

LEECH, JOHN (1817-1864)

Educated at the Charterhouse; formed friendship there with W. M. Thackeray. Studied
medicine for a time at St. Bartholomew's.
Worked for *Punch* as chief political cartoonist
from 1841 until his death. Among his best
novel illustrations are drawings for novels by
R. S. Surtees.

MACLISE, DANIEL (1806-1870)

Best known as an historical painter. Entered
the Royal Academy schools in 1828. Began
exhibiting at the Academy in 1829. Became
acquainted with Dickens in 1830; contributed
illustrations to Dickens' *Master Humphrey's
Clock* (1840-41) and several of the Christmas
books.

MILLAIS, SIR JOHN EVERETT (1829-1896)

Entered Royal Academy schools in 1840; first
exhibited at the Academy in 1846. In 1848
originated with Holman Hunt the pre-Raphaelite

movement. Among his best novel illustrations
were those for Anthony Trollope's *Framley
Parsonage* (1860-61), *Orley Farm* (1861-62), *The
Small House at Allington* (1862-64) and *Phineas
Finn* (1867-69).

ONWHYN, THOMAS (?-1886)

Early in his career prepared a series of un-
authorized illustrations to the works of
Dickens. Contributed illustrations to novels
by Henry Cockton, Charles Selby and Eugène Sue.

SEYMOUR, ROBERT (?1800-1836)

Illustrated Ovid, Shakespeare, Wordsworth,
Southey. Prepared drawings for two parts of
Dickens' *The Pickwick Papers.*

THACKERAY, WILLIAM MAKEPEACE (1811-1863)

Educated at Charterhouse and at Trinity
College, Cambridge. In 1831 began study of
law, then studied art briefly in Paris. Comic
journalist and reviewer in the 1830s and
1840s. Illustrated much of his own fiction.

WALKER, FREDERICK (1840-1875)

Prolific book illustrator. Collaborated with
W. M. Thackeray on *The Adventures of Philip*
(1861-62) and *Denis Duval* (1864).

INDEXES

Index of Authors

References are to entry numbers.

General Index

A Beckett, Gilbert, 270.

*Alice's Adventures in Won-
    derland*, 192, 204, 262,
    317.

Air;worth, W. Harrison,
    20, 26, 92; Biblio-
    graphy, 53.

Barnaby Rudge, 183, 216,
    307.

Blackmore, R. D., 133.

Bleak House, 127, 183,
    220, 245, 263, 270.

Book Illustration; Biblio-
    graphy, 163, 166, 170,
    190, 292; General Dis-
    cussion, 9, 30, 46, 47,
    58, 59, 64, 73, 81, 82,
    97, 105, 107, 108, 110,
    117, 119, 126, 128, 146,
    151, 161, 173, 174, 180,
    181, 184, 186, 199, 200,
    208, 211, 212, 225, 232,
    235, 241, 248, 253, 257,
    271, 284, 316, 318.

Browne, H. K., 4, 15, 17,
    26, 29, 34, 35, 45, 79,
    89, 90, 125, 136, 139,
    201, 228, 235, 307;
    Bibliography, 177.

Buss, R. W., 18, 24, 26,
    77, 88, 90.

Caricature, 85, 228.

Carroll, Lewis, 182, 192,
    310, 317.

Cattermole, George, 15,
    233, 307.

Children's Book Illustration,
    76, 131, 147, 155, 167.

Christmas Books, Charles
    Dickens', 93, 113, 210,
    287, 315.

Clark, J. Clayton, 134.

Collins, Charles, 43, 66,
    261, 276, 301.

Collins, Wilkie; Biblio-
    graphy, 176.

Crane, Walter, 305.

Cranford, 159, 169.

Cruikshank, George, 15, 17,
    18, 20, 26, 42, 49, 63,
    70, 92, 100, 106, 121,
    124, 153, 221, 223, 235,
    249, 250, 256, 273, 274,
    275, 278, 279, 280, 282,
    285, 288, 289, 294, 297,